Coaching for Impact

The world is changing. The first century of the third millennium has seen exponential growth and advancement in almost all areas, and makes the last century of the second millennium look like a rusty old steam train by comparison.

The "digital revolution" is no longer a revolution. Practically anyone can publicise their outlook, whilst having access to a wealth of information at the click of a button. And this levels out the playing field in an unprecedented and unpredictable way.

So how can anyone stand out? How can anyone gain a competitive advantage? How can anyone master more *influence*?

How can anyone *lead*?

The answer lies in coaching: a discipline that enhances performance by generating meaning through the art of relating.

In *Coaching for Impact*, Vassilis Antonas brings together his dual expertise in executive coaching and psychotherapy to present a transformative, evolutionary approach. The book examines methodology, presence and fundamental skills and includes a new, innovative model of leadership. Antonas also uses Jungian concepts to address the coach's internal disposition, supporting their evolution and transformation.

Coaching for Impact equips trainee and beginner coaches with an A to Z of executive coaching and engages seasoned practitioners in an uncompromised pursuit of excellence by pushing the boundaries of leadership coaching. It will appeal to executive and leadership coaches at all levels, including those in training.

Vassilis Antonas is an Executive Coach, Psychotherapist, Organisational Development Consultant and Course Director of Impact's Diploma in Executive Coaching and Organisational Development (AADCT). He has consulted internationally for a wide range of functions and industries.

Coaching for Impact

The Evolution of Leadership

Vassilis Antonas

Routledge
Taylor & Francis Group

LONDON AND NEW YORK

First published 2018
by Routledge
2 Park Square, Milton Park, Abingdon, Oxon OX14 4RN

and by Routledge
711 Third Avenue, New York, NY 10017

Routledge is an imprint of the Taylor & Francis Group, an informa business

© 2018 Vassilis Antonas

The right of Vassilis Antonas to be identified as author of this work
has been asserted by him in accordance with sections 77 and 78 of
the Copyright, Designs and Patents Act 1988.

British Library Cataloguing in Publication Data
A catalogue record for this book is available from the British Library.

Library of Congress Cataloging in Publication Data
Names: Antonas, Vassilis, author.
Title: Coaching for impact / Vassilis Antonas.
Description: Abingdon, Oxon; New York, NY : Routledge, 2018.
Identifiers: LCCN 2017023954 (print) | LCCN 2017037572 (ebook) |
ISBN 9781315110400 (Master E-Book) | ISBN 9781138087569
(hardback) | ISBN 9781138087576 (pbk.)
Subjects: LCSH: Executive coaching.
Classification: LCC HD30.4 (ebook) |
LCC HD30.4.A628 2018 (print) | DDC 658.4/07124—dc23
LC record available at https://lccn.loc.gov/2017023954

ISBN: 978-1-138-08756-9 (hbk)
ISBN: 978-1-138-08757-6 (pbk)
ISBN: 978-1-315-11040-0 (ebk)

Typeset in Times New Roman
by Keystroke, Neville Lodge, Tettenhall, Wolverhampton

Contents

Preface

The purpose of this book[1] is twofold: First, it aims to provide trainee and beginner coaches with an A to Z of executive coaching. Second, it aspires to engage seasoned practitioners beyond that, in an uncompromised pursuit of excellence by pushing the boundaries of coaching further. This entails taking the risk of, once they have been presented, putting the manuals and cook books aside and appreciating that the coachee cannot travel further into uncharted territory than the coach.

Executive coaching is a very young discipline that has flourished over the past couple of decades, for the most part due to the market's increasing demand for it, the establishment of solid training programs and some initial research. Its methodological underpinnings can be found in the behavioural sciences (psychology), business and, of course, sport; its theoretical origins can be traced as far back as Ancient Greece; its ultimate aim of maximising performance for winners clearly resonates well within the realms of military endeavours also. However, anyone who feels that an adequate understanding of just one of the aforementioned themes will suffice in rendering them an expert in the field of coaching is sorely mistaken. The reason is fairly straightforward: The whole is greater than the sum of its parts.

Business people and executives need to supplement their expertise with the psychological background required to bring about change; behavioural scientists need to appreciate that the quest for meaning (that is effectively the primary driver for psychotherapy) needs to be combined with supporting performance and even profitability; academics and theoreticians need to be able to transfer their knowledge towards an applicable direction; sports figures (including sports coaches) need to acquire the necessary tools (language, business principles, etc.) to effectively convey their message to their teams. The ability to integrate the new, whilst maintaining the existing, is vital. It's a *transformational process*.

It was with the above in my (subconscious) mind that, more than a decade ago (2004), together with Bernd Leygraf, I co-founded the Diploma in Executive Coaching and Organisational Development, a coaching training course that successfully runs in London through the Naos Institute and in Athens via Impact. The course is open to all of the aforementioned categories of candidates (and more) and integrates theoretical and practical coaching components in a way that provides each and every participant with a competitive edge. At the same time, it aligns tools with skills, behaviours with internal growth, performance with meaning and, finally, doing with being.

The evolution of this training program, which was globally the very first to be accredited by the Association for Coaching in 2014, as brought about by facilitators and participants alike, coupled, primarily, with my accumulated know-how as a consultant for more than 60 local and multinational firms over the last decade and supported by my work as a psychotherapist over the last two decades, is what I will be sharing with the reader of this book. I know it's a long, breathless sentence. It's been a long, breathless ride. Thank you for coming along.

Note

1 Unless otherwise stated, all quotes included in this book originate with the author.

Acknowledgements

For the evolution of this text, I would like to thank:

- My trainer of almost 10 years and currently friend and colleague, Bernd Leygraf, for laying the foundations for both my psychotherapy and coaching practice;
- my supervisor, Professor Renos Papadopoulos, for repeatedly demonstrating to me that I am miles behind from where I think I am – and that I can't cut corners in the pursuit of excellence;
- my former business partner and business mentor at CAP London, Ian Brown, for ascertaining that helping others adds enough value to come with fair remuneration;
- my late Sociology Professor, Dimitris Carmocolias, for demonstrating that I should do what I am – and not vice versa;
- my mother, Anna, and my father, Antonis, for providing me with enough confidence to go for it and enough prudence to keep it real;
- my friend, colleague and alumnus, George Mavros, who spoke to me one hour ago (2014) and said, "start with the acknowledgments and the foreword" and who returned the edited first draft to me last night (2016);
- my former wife, and alumna, Maria, for always and often wrongly convincing me I can fly;
- my friend, colleague and alumnus, Dr George Diakonikolaou, who consistently maintained and nurtured our relationship;
- my friend, colleague and alumnus, Paul Kidner, for his integrity and spirit;
- my first Associate at Impact, Magda Hatzidimitri, for her warm professionalism;
- my friend and colleague, Jaap Westerbos, for always pointing out the reverse side of the reverse side;
- my friend and alumnus, Michael Boussias, who supported Impact and myself with his publications and conferences over the past decade;
- my friend, piano coach and alumna, Katerina Nikoloutsou, for widening my thinking patterns;

- each and every participant of the Diploma in Executive Coaching and Organisational Development over the past 10 years, in Athens and London, each for a different reason;
- my team at Impact for their loyalty, performance and integrity;
- my assistant, Mrs Ismini Kakoura Varakli (MIKV), for patiently supporting me with editing the manuscript;
- Sun Tzu, Carl von Clausewitz, Ernesto Che Guevara, Niccolò Machiavelli, Yamamoto Tsunetomo, Alexander and every strategist who confirmed it is not a sin to strive for victory;
- the late Stephen Covey for producing the blueprint of all coaching texts, *The 7 Habits of Highly Effective People*, and for saying to me, "keep thinking win–win" on a spring afternoon in 2008;
- Carl Gustav Jung, for everything;
- each and every one of my corporate clients from more than 60 multinational and Greek companies who took the risk of trusting me, even when they could not fully understand me;
- each and every one of my private coaching and therapy clients who taught me something new in each session;
- everyone who judged and criticised me – especially those whose own track record convinced me that I was on the right track;
- everyone who gave me courageous and honest feedback with the intention of helping me improve.

Introduction

Influence: The ability and capacity to deliberately determine, increase and direct your transformational impact at your own pace.

The world is changing. The first century of the third millennium has seen exponential growth and advancement in almost all areas; and makes the last century of the second millennium look like a rusty old steam train by comparison.

On influence

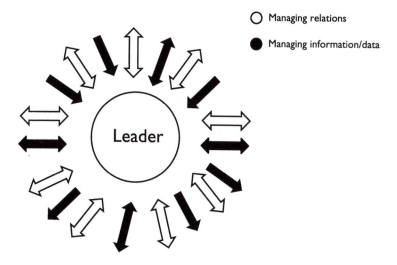

O Managing relations

● Managing information/data

Figure 0.1 Model of Influence

The "digital revolution" is no longer a revolution: With almost two-thirds of the world's population using a mobile phone and almost half (49.5%) having access to the Internet (Kemp, 2017; Wikipedia, 2016: 'Digital revolution'), the revolution has now become the established norm. In the Western world, access to a "smart phone" is gradually and steadily becoming mandatory. The ease and pace at which *information* is transmitted has diminished the time required to get things done to an unprecedented minimum. The few seconds it has taken me to collect the above information, compared to the minutes, perhaps hours, it would have taken me to do the same thing for my high school project in the 1980s, is proof enough.

At the same time, the 21st century saw the earth's population rise from approximately 6 billion to 7 billion. Medical advancements and higher standards of living probably mean that a further 50% rise by 2050 is a strong possibility (UN Population Division). It is not difficult to deduce that, eventually, we will be very hard pressed to match the demand for energy, food and other *resources*, as the ease with which we extract and secure them increases; until, of course, we run out.

However, this text is neither about information technology nor about the tremendous challenge of managing environmental resources. It is about *relating and leading*. So how do these three seemingly separate aspects share common ground? And most importantly, what is their association with executive coaching?

The answer to the above questions has at least two dimensions.

The quest for optimum performance has always greatly depended on the amount and quality of *influence* one can secure. As far as I am concerned, *influence is determined by our ability to collect and utilise information, access and secure resources and manage relations*. With information becoming increasingly and routinely available and resources becoming increasingly scarce, *managing relations suddenly appears as the competitive advantage that will separate those who sustainably succeed from those who merely survive.*

In addition, as automated functions continue to make the human contribution to productivity increasingly obsolete, *the primary qualities that organisations, corporations and governments will seek from their people, will be those that machines and automated functions cannot produce: relational and leadership skills.*

On evolution

Based on the above, it is fairly safe to assume that the individuals who master the art and craft of relating and leading for themselves and for others, namely professionals with coaching expertise as this book will propose, will gradually, increasingly and steadily become an extremely valuable commodity. Over the past couple of decades, the business world appears to be grasping this reality.

The shift in allocating budgets from technical training for executives to supporting their "soft" skills is fairly evident – as is the tendency to finally replace the word "soft" with the word "leadership". The era of the executive who awkwardly rose to a management position by merit of their technical expertise is bidding us farewell. Corporations demand more, a lot more. At the same time, leadership-training providers (internal and external) have had to pick up their game and have moved from mere ready-made "tin can" training programs to sophisticated, tailor-made programs for teams and individuals. Companies and corporations, with access to a practically unlimited database (information) of leadership consultants, trainers and coaches and very limited access to money (resources) are on the constant lookout for the approach, method and individual who will provide them with the best value for money when it comes to investing in their human capital (relating). It is the theory of *evolution* and the survival of those able to adapt all over again. There is no question, these are tough times (for corporations and consultants alike) and natural selection will admonish those unwilling to evolve; this is where this book comes in.

On coaches

> Separating fulfilment from achievement is the new age cop out from both.

Several people indicate that coaching originates back in Ancient Greece; and probably, rightly so. *Socrates* gave us *maieutics*, a dialogue whereby two parties exchange thoughts, ideas and opinions with the aim of proving their point. The process itself, a process of questioning everything and staying sharp, is an integral part of what coaching, *evocative* coaching in particular, ought to be. This method is about being the devil's advocate, something that a seasoned coach should include in their arsenal of interventions.

Aristotle's syllogism promoted the concept of deductive reasoning, which, despite its presumption of assumptions, is the quickest logical route anyone can follow to reach conclusions. The method works via a simple 3-step process. For example, all coaches value performance. John is a coach. John values performance. This is a somewhat more *provocative* approach.

Plato's theory of forms is yet another attempt to explore and discover the truth, albeit in a somewhat more abstract manner than Aristotle. Plato argues that everything has one true core, origin and nature, a *blueprint* so to speak; and from then on, this blueprint reincarnates itself in various, less perfect forms. The original, however, remains pure, perfect and unchanging.

As you can probably gather, and despite the inexorable links, it would be somewhat difficult to coach based on Greek philosophy alone. Coaching draws heavily from these concepts, and no doubt the astute reader will be able to identify them throughout the text, be it in Chapter 4: Fundamental skills: "Psychodynamic competencies and the use of self"; "Process versus content"; and "Giving and receiving feedback"; Chapter 5: Transformational leadership: "The Archetype and Individuation" and in several other places. However, the fact remains that coaching intervenes within a stricter, narrower methodological context; and as such, it needs to be treated as *a young and new discipline in its own right*, currently transforming its own plot. There is no doubt that philosophers, such as the aforementioned, have provided practically the totality of our building materials; however, the fact remains that we are still in the process of trying to figure out how to put them together and this provides room for opportunity as well as threats and risks.

Executive coaches need to be versatile, multidimensional, balanced in their expertise and approach and self-aware, to mention just a few of the required characteristics (we will be expanding on those at a later stage in this text). Anyone who thinks they can just step in and make the transition into this discipline (and I purposively avoid the term profession for reasons that we will again explore later) is in for a surprise. Retired executives, experienced psychotherapists, sports figures, academics, former management consultants and others, who felt that their existing experience and expertise sufficed, have tried; and failed.

With demand for excellence and value for money becoming the norm in what corporations expect when hiring an executive coach (or utilising an internal one), the past few years have seen a great number of "visitors" and "passers-by" wrap up their business (or resort to more manageable, unregulated and ambiguous approaches such as "life coaching"). The restriction in resources and budgets is unforgiving and inevitably promotes selectivity. It is slowly yet steadily established that coaching is a discipline in its own right, and should one wish to master it, then hard work and study are required in equal measure. There are no free passes any more.

This book has been written in order to support those who understand this.

On coaching

As indicated in the very first paragraph of this book, my aim extends beyond providing the trainee or beginner coach with a coaching blueprint. I wish to contribute towards the evolution of our discipline by inviting seasoned practitioners to step beyond the safety of our tools and methodologies, into the unknown; the unknown of using the *self* as the primary agent of transformation.

Let's kick off with my proposed definition of executive coaching: *"The theory and practice of an agent of transformation, supporting a professional's awareness, leadership and talent, through behavioural and business interventions, within an organisational context."*

Almost each word carries weight and meaning and I would like us to painstakingly dissect the above statement in order to start shedding some light on the path that will reveal itself over the next few pages.

*"**The theory and practice** of an agent of transformation, supporting a professional's awareness, leadership and talent, through behavioural and business interventions, within an organisational context."* The term "theory" has received a lot of criticism in recent years, at best from new age "progressives" and at worst from people who are too lazy to read or study. It would, however, be a gross misjudgement from our side to choose not to contribute towards the development

of an Epistemology for coaching. Even though its ancestors will always be psychology, business and sport, in order to stand firmly, we need to contribute towards its individuation with adequate research, theory generation and the establishment of an academic backbone. This is slowly taking place and alongside the offered professional training programs, several universities are now providing coaching programs at Master's level. Needless to say, we need to put our findings to the test through practice, which we should, in turn, document in the form of case studies.

*"The theory and practice of **an agent of transformation**, supporting a professional's awareness, leadership and talent, through behavioural and business interventions, within an organisational context."* In recent years, I have come to realise that describing myself as an "agent of change" not only sounded fairly arrogant, but also created unrealistic expectations from both my coachees and myself. At the end of the day, as coaches, we work with the material that is available (both within an organisational as well as an individual context) and willing it to change into something good rather than transform into something *even* better is not, in my humble opinion, the way of coaching.

*"The theory and practice of an agent of transformation, **supporting a professional's awareness, leadership and talent**, through behavioural and business interventions, within an organisational context."* The three elements mentioned here are pretty much in order of importance. *Awareness* refers primarily to our ability to recognise the impact we have on others and secondarily to acknowledge our set of values, opinions, limiting beliefs, etc. It is clearly a prerequisite to *leading*, since an understanding of the impact we have on others gives us the opportunity to match our intention with outcome; and this generates confidence, inspiration, loyalty and several other key leadership characteristics. Finally, the coach supports the coachee by identifying and utilising areas of strength (*talent*) in order to generate circumstances for progression.

*"The theory and practice of an agent of transformation, supporting a professional's awareness, leadership and talent, through **behavioural** and business interventions, within an organisational context."* Even though I am choosing not to use the term psychological, this is effectively what I am referring to when referring to behaviour. My choice comes as a result of my intention to separate psychotherapy from coaching, because, despite their close relation, the former deals with *generating **meaning*** and the latter with *optimising **performance***. Nonetheless, coaching entails a strong psychological component, in the context of understanding *why* things happen, but most importantly with regard to *the purpose they serve*. Needless to say, we will explore this theme extensively throughout this text. For the time being, it should suffice to underline that an executive coach with no psychology expertise will find it difficult to produce sustainable results. Most respectable coaching training programs should have adequate backbone when it comes to "ψ" ("psy") expertise.

*"The theory and practice of an agent of transformation, supporting a professional's awareness, leadership and talent, through behavioural and **business***

interventions, within an organisational context." The business aspect of executive coaching carries at least equal weight to the psychological. Providing executive coaching services without the understanding that your job is to generate added value and profit within a commercial setting is at best unprofessional and at worst unethical.

Even though it is not the coach's job to provide management, strategy or financial consulting services, one should aim to have a fair understanding of how the corporate world goes around. Even if you originate from a psychology background, as I do, in due time, your engagement with multinationals and corporations will strengthen your understanding of business concepts. However, you need to have proactively secured that in advance. An executive coach who does not originate from a business background should read up on publications such as the *Harvard Business Review*, *The Economist*, the *Financial Times*, etc., aim to talk to as many people in business as they can, attend a relevant training program and get acquainted with the corporate beast.

"The theory and practice of an agent of transformation, supporting a professional's awareness, leadership and talent, through behavioural and business interventions, within an **organisational context.***"* This final point has been and will continue to be a subject for debate. Several coaches argue that you do not require organisational development expertise to provide executive coaching services. I could not personally disagree more. Even when coaching a self-funded entrepreneur or executive, your aim is to empower them into becoming an invaluable asset for their business or organisation. This is even more the case when you are coaching a company-funded executive. The aim of the coach is not only to improve the executive's individual performance; it is *to align the executive's performance with the organisational strategy, mission and vision*. Therefore your ability to secure a solid understanding of the *system of* which your coachee is part is non-negotiable. I cannot simplify this more. Neglect the development of your systemic, organisational expertise and understanding at your own and your client's risk.

On coaching for impact

The coach needs to be versatile, multidimensional, dynamic, perceptive, organised, skilful, present, authentic . . . the list goes on. I wish to use this text as a medium for conveying the numerous challenges and as a support towards facing them. One of the most exigent aspects of writing was the organisation of data. Having authored and directed two coaching training programs over the past decade, my assumption was that transferring the data from the training setting into a book would be fairly straightforward. It has been anything but. During the training, a simple heading or even a picture will suffice to stimulate discussion, reflection and exploration that will render the topic comprehensible. These liberties afforded by the interactive element are not provided here. Diagrams (which are used throughout the text) proved to be the best answer. Contrary to coaching, which focuses on the coachee, this book focuses primarily on the coach. The coach features four dimensions, which ought to be developed equally:

1 *Skills:* The first and possibly most straightforward aspect of becoming a coach is learning what to do. Skills include active listening, giving feedback, creating rapport and collecting data (the latter also overlaps as part of the method). This is also the tip of the iceberg in terms of what the coach delivers and what the coachee directly receives.
2 *Method:* This is the first of the two cornerstones of a seasoned coach and it refers to the school(s) of thought they adhere to, their basic project management system, contracting, reporting, etc.
3 *Presence:* This is the second cornerstone for coaching practice and it encompasses our way of being as others perceive this. Pace, body language and use of language as well as more subtle and complex characteristics (such as balance) fall under this category.
4 *Disposition:* This, in my opinion, is the aspect that differentiates a brilliant coach from a very good practitioner. Our internal state of affairs, based on our self-awareness, willingness to take risks, capacity to be available and ability to generate and convey *meaning*, are all aspects of our disposition. Even though this is not directly visible to the coachee, it is nonetheless a determining factor in the success of the engagement.

Figure 0.2 outlines the aforementioned dimensions. Separate chapters will be allocated for each property and its subdivisions.

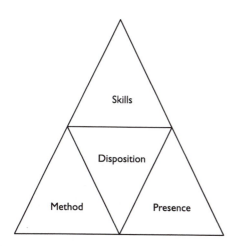

Figure 0.2 The coach

On the coachee: Three dimensions to consider

The second facet of this book is going to be dealing with the coachee. Some representative case studies will be employed to shed some light on the identity of what is effectively our subject matter, since people come in all "shapes and sizes" and unlike the coach, do not have to stick to any guidelines. The case studies will focus mostly on challenges, shortcomings and the learning curve rather than triumphant textbook success stories. I feel this will prove far more valuable to the reader.

Coachees can do as they please, and for the most part, they exercise this right. They can be as resistant, stubborn, argumentative and uncooperative as they wish. At this point, it is of course worth mentioning that we are not obligated to work with every coachee who is assigned to us (chemistry is also a consideration); however, *it is the most adverse cases that result in our most profound development.* If I had two personal prerequisites when choosing to work with someone, it is that they have been identified as having *high potential* and are *voluntarily engaging* in the coaching process. When it comes to the rest, pretty much anything goes.

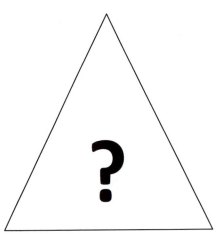

Figure 0.3 The coachee

At the same time, it is worth "beginning with the end in mind" (Covey, 1989, p. 97) and what comes to my mind when I read the definition of executive coaching is that as consultants we are invited to work with our clients on three levels:

1   *Awareness:* This is our primary task. If we all knew how we are perceived, we would be in a position to do something about it – *or choose not to.* The same goes if we had conscious and clear access to our beliefs (limiting and others) and the way these shape our behaviour.
2   *Behaviour:* Once you support your coachee's awareness, it is up to them to decide on their action plan, or employ your support in devising one. You may

want to help your client consider the pros and cons (or the P and L, Profit and Loss) of changing, and if they decide that change is in their interest, then you can help them devise and implement an appropriate, alternative behavioural intervention.

3   *Skills:* This certainly does not refer to technical skills. This is the job of a mentor (debate about what constitutes mentoring and what constitutes coaching has been going on for years, and despite the meaning that each one of us attributes to the terms, using them interchangeably to describe the same thing shows great lack of expertise and understanding, in my opinion). It refers to your coachee's ability to lead, motivate, empower, delegate and above all optimise performance for themselves as well as for others. This is a focused area for intervention and Chapters 7 (Coaching team managers) and 8 (Leading with PRAID) will address the issue of equipping your coachees with leadership and management skills extensively.

Figure 0.4 The coachee II

And finally, perhaps we ought to consider the ways in which the coachee is a reflection of the coach and vice versa. Consider this reality every time you are tempted to teach and train rather than facilitate and coach.

On the coaching relation

The third component of the coaching process, the space within which the coach and the client meet and conduct the work, is the relation itself. This is the *co-created field. This space needs to be as much about safety as it is about taking risks; as much about support as it is about challenge; as much about synergising as it is about individuating.* A third, new entity is created with the purpose of hosting a meaningful and productive encounter. The conscious and unconscious aspects and dimensions of the coach (skills, disposition, beliefs, etc.) come in contact with the conscious and unconscious aspects and dimensions of the coachee. Even though the client is the protagonist in this process, if this *alchemical connection*

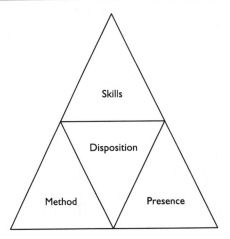

Figure 0.5 The coachee. The coach

is powerful and meaningful enough, then both parties should leave the relation *transformed* at the end. I will not elaborate further on this encounter here, since, effectively, this is the central theme of this text and the next few chapters will explore it extensively.

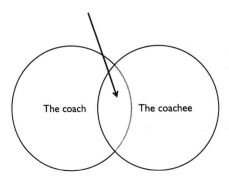

Figure 0.6 The co-created coaching field

Chapter 1

Becoming a coach

> Take your eyes off the problem ... don't even focus on the solution. Just seek the opportunity.

Whereas there is a fair amount of literature on how to coach, some of it particularly good, I feel some other questions are slightly overlooked, avoided or even sugar coated under a thin, politically correct frosting of "anyone can coach" or something to that effect. It may sound harsh; however, coaching is not for everybody, it is not suitable for all circumstances, it *can* be done in the wrong way and timing matters. Below I will try to present some answers, as my experience and expertise dictate, on four important questions, which you may wish to also ask yourselves before reading on, especially if you have not yet fully committed to becoming an executive coach: Who, why, when and how?

Who can become an executive coach?

> "I'm (chronically) vulnerable", eventually turns into a blackmailing mandate; compelling that one's emotion, controls another's behaviour.

I find it easier to begin answering this question in an anticlockwise direction. Who should not become an executive coach? Psychotherapists whose sole reason for moving into the corporate world is to supplement their income; counsellors who perceive the notion of profitability or even success as anathema; leftists, anarchists and anachronistic socialists (in the confined, absolutist sense of the terms) who feel the same, *unless* they feel they can offer their services to non-governmental organisations (NGOs), "for good" organisations, charities, etc. (which is a beautiful thing); executives who have hit a hard wall in their career and are driven by desperation; "romantics" or those wearing the Persona of a romantic, who just want to "help someone" and/or "change the world", when in fact all they are craving is a few crumbs of authority (fortunately and despite all the risks it poses, "life coaching" has absorbed the majority of these individuals); anyone who feels that their existing knowledge and expertise, regardless of the level of proficiency, will suffice to practise coaching and that there is no need for further training; anyone who practises coaching after a couple of weekend seminars. The list could go on; however, I am confident that by now you get the point.

So, who does that leave? It leaves *all of the above and many more*, provided that they re-examine their motives and fulfil the criteria listed below. See if you can recognise yourself:

1 *You strongly believe in unlocking potential and optimising performance:* (If you find yourself questioning or philosophising around the terms "potential" and "performance", then you may be suitable for a career that focuses more on *meaning* and *fulfilment* [such as counselling or "life coaching"]). Even though executive coaching takes these factors seriously into consideration, performance remains its primary deliverable. For those still wondering, performance in the corporate world is numerically assessed and it means bigger, better, faster and any other comparative, which will put the executive and their organisation in the driver's seat and maximise influence.

2 *You have undertaken some personal work, which has generated sufficient self-awareness:* We all come with our set of assumptions, limiting beliefs, (please see Chapter 4: Fundamental skills: "Generating data": "The Gestalt Cycle": Introjects), bias, principles, etc. We will be leaking and projecting some of those onto our clients, no matter what and this will have a considerable impact on our work. The important thing is to keep this distortion within a manageable context, employ damage limitation and perhaps even use who we are to the advantage of the coachee. Since the enhancement of awareness and self-awareness is a fundamental aspect of coaching (any kind of coaching), we need to be able to model this effectively and implicitly by walking the talk. Most serious coaching training programs incorporate a fundamental element of self-exploration even though for those wishing to take matters even further, personal psychotherapy or psychoanalysis can provide an even richer, wider, solid base and I strongly recommend it for coaches who take their work seriously.

3 *You have a basic understanding of psychological principles:* This does not necessarily mean being a qualified psychologist, psychotherapist or counsellor. Even though such qualifications can give you a head start in one direction, they may constrict you in another, as already discussed. At the same time, you need a basic understanding of "what gets people going", an ability to read between the lines and beyond the obvious and the capacity to separate *process from content* (please see Chapter 4: Fundamental skills: "Generating data": "Psychodynamic competencies and the use of self": "Process versus content").

4 *You have a fair grasp of business principles:* Again, this does not necessarily restrict coaching to those from a business background, though it can be just

as helpful as having a background in psychology. Executive coaching aims primarily at increasing performance in order to increase profitability. Understanding how a business works and coming to terms with its commercial nature is of the essence.

5   *You value being proactive over troubleshooting:* Many consultants thrive on having to tackle problems and being able to provide solutions. Coaching is a different ballgame altogether. You support the generation of data for your client and then you proceed to share the accountability of co-creating alternative, multidimensional and transformational interventions. *It is a frame of mind rather than a skill set and in some ways this is what this book is all about.* This is also the reason why I would encourage coaches to consider themselves as consultants with executive coaching skills rather than professional executive coaches. Therefore . . .

6   *You view individuals as part of a system rather than an isolated entity:* This consideration separates the coach who can improve an individual from the coach who can create real added value for the company that recruits them. In order to be able to understand your coachee, their role, their needs and their required contribution within the corporation, you need to obtain a solid understanding of the organisation. Your primary task as a coach is to align your executive's performance with their organisation's strategy. In order to do that you need to be able to access organisational data (by establishing and maintaining contact with key stakeholders); you need to secure sufficient authority to be able to implement your proposals; and you need to have the know-how to be able to do so for the benefit of the system. *It is my opinion that a coach is first and foremost an* **Organisational Development Consultant**, and even though this text focuses on the individual's development within an organisation, the material will be presented with a systemic predisposition in mind.

Why become an executive coach?

The previous section partly presented my thoughts on why you should *not* become an executive coach. There are, however, several good reasons as to why you should. For a start, the fundamentals for a great career (job satisfaction, work environment, pay rate and progression prospects) provide potential for excellence. More specifically:

- Supporting people's growth and improvement is a noble cause and amounts to tons of job satisfaction.
- It is just as suitable for people wanting to change their career as it is for people who want to stay in it. Coaching is first and foremost a skill and therefore can be as useful to an executive as to a consultant.
- For an executive, it clearly increases influence. People will flock around you to benefit from the ways you can help them. In addition, you learn how to get things done easier, faster, sustainably and overall more effectively.

- For a freelancer, it encompasses all the benefits of being independent: control over your working hours, absence of a boss (though an increase in the number of people you will be reporting to) and fewer excuses regarding the internal politics and circumstances, which inhibit your career progress.
- You do not need to give up what you are doing. This is a huge advantage for a multitude of reasons: You (and your clients) continue to benefit from your existing expertise (for example, your mental health, management consulting or business background) and you can maintain your existing flow of income, thus risking less from a sudden career change.
- As a freelancer, it will not get boring. There is rotation in your work environment, colleagues, objectives, approach and methodology and challenges.
- As an executive, it will not get boring either: Coaching opens up a multitude of aspects and dimensions and generates potential and momentum which can be an excellent source of new-found interest in one's work.
- Coaching training for executives is an express ride on the train of career advancement. I have carefully observed the career progress of more than 100 of our training's alumni and I can testify and substantiate that their rate of ascent is much faster than that of the average executive. Middle management are now in C-level positions (e.g. CEO, CFO) and C-level executives hold regional posts or are part of the company's central HQ.
- The pay rate can be very satisfactory. As a beginner (provided you have completed substantial training and your practice hours), your rate per session should feature three digits. As your career progresses, an hourly rate of a few or several hundred Euros, Pounds or Dollars is not unreasonable. The hourly rate for top coaches in developed markets can reach a few thousand Euros per session. In addition, conducting sessions via web conference, therefore gaining global access and charging global rates, is certainly possible.

When should you become an executive coach?

Timing is of the essence in almost everything we do in life. Coaching is no exception. My personal opinion is that the best time to engage with your coaching training is once you have successfully established yourself in your existing career, which for most of us amounts to approximately a decade from when we started. This renders your move a proactive quest for excellence. Going at it because you are nearing burnout, because your compromised performance got you fired or because you want to "help" people, but can't be bothered with the long clinical training required to become a therapist constitute your choice one of necessity; and that surely can't stand as good timing. Approaching coaching as the panacea to all your troubles (personal or professional) is also not a great idea.

At the same time, it is your internal state of affairs (i.e., how you interpret what is happening for you rather than what is actually happening) which makes choices right – or wrong. However, a certain level of professional and personal maturity is required if you are to help others improve. For instance, I would be hesitant to recruit a 23 year old, with a couple of years of work experience and a fragile sense of self and direction, on Impact's Diploma course, simply because they are eager to gain some kind of credential or accreditation (a profile which accounts for approximately 10% of the applications we receive [and of course reject] each year for the Diploma). We maintain a cut-off point of 25 years of age, though in reality we have never recruited anyone under 30.

I trust and hope that the three previous sections (who, why and when) have challenged and supported all those interested in following the coach's path in equal measure. So if you are still reading, here are the basics of *how* to equip yourself for the job.

How do you become an executive coach?

Before presenting some of the practicalities, it is worth paying attention to the required frame of mind. The seasoned coach will eventually place emphasis on "being" rather than "doing". Even though once it becomes natural, it is difficult to regress, achieving this type of presence requires time and the travelling of signifi-cant distance – not to mention the necessity of "getting it wrong" several times. Neurolinguistic Programming (NLP) practitioners advocate that knowledge is achieved in four stages: unconscious incompetence, conscious incompetence, conscious competence and unconscious competence.

I feel that it is particularly useful for the apprentice coach to begin their journey with this in mind. The first stage, *unconscious incompetence*, is our natural state of being in relation to any craft that we have not studied – and should be taken as a given. The second stage occurs once we accumulate the minimum expertise required to provide us with an understanding of the amount of work required to

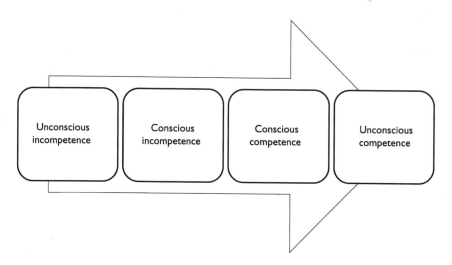

Figure 1.1 Four stages of competence

achieve excellence. Experts in all fields return to the *conscious incompetence* stage very frequently and respectfully work towards their goals as if stuck there. Being aware of what you cannot do is vital and is the only way to pursue optimum performance.

Conscious competence is the most honest and straightforward stage. It consists of applying knowledge in an orderly and structured way so that it creates a fairly predictable outcome. The trainee coach's anxiety to accumulate various tools (such as profilers), techniques (such as GROW; see Whitmore, 2009, p. 55) and methodologies (such as the solution-focused approach) is not only natural, but also pretty much mandatory. This is the place to start and even though this will not be our focus (the Internet and relevant bibliography render this topic easily accessible), we will still be sharing some, for the most part "homemade", tools. However, it is worth noting that the seasoned consultant's preoccupation with them usually reflects a need to find shelter from uncertainty; and in my opinion, can only account for an acceptable outcome within a coaching engagement and rarely for an outstanding one. An easy way to identify such consultants is simply to observe whether their promotional material focuses primarily on announcing the superiority of the particular tool they happen to be using, as opposed to how they will integrate their knowledge for the benefit of their client.

The final stage, *unconscious competence*, is pure magic in the making. It is strongly associated with the stage of conscious incompetence and even though my co-patriot Socrates summarised it well by infamously yet allegedly stating, "I know one thing; that I know nothing", Yamamoto Tsunetomo (1659–1719), a samurai author, expanded appropriately on this topic in a way that I feel will be particularly useful to the trainee coach:

> In the highest level a man has the look of knowing nothing. These are the levels in general; but there is one transcending level, and this is the most excellent of all. This person is aware of the endlessness of entering deeply into a certain Way and never thinks of himself as having finished. He truly knows his own insufficiencies and never in his whole life thinks that he has succeeded.
>
> (Tsunetomo, 1979, p. 32)

In addition to being rather than doing, for executive coaching, the *way* partly lies in being able to naturally *separate content from process*, since it is, in my opinion, the distinguishing factor between a "good enough" coach and a coach who offers excellence.

Having looked at the required development continuum that enables one to be an executive coach, let's focus on the *training* that equips one with coaching skills. As mentioned earlier, previous experience and expertise in business, mental health or consulting will not suffice. Neither will a weekend seminar or a collection of weekend seminars for that matter. A specialised, focused yet multifaceted training lasting at least *100 hours* over a period of at least *6 months* is, in my opinion, the absolute minimum starting point. The course syllabus and content should include and cover:

- *At least two different coaching methodologies:* (Gestalt, solution-focused, NLP, psychodynamic, etc). I want to underline that simple tools (such as GROW) are not a method.
- *A systemic perspective:* This will provide the coach with at least some organisational development competencies. The lack of such a component will render the coach immeasurably less effective, since what we are getting paid for is the *alignment of individual performance with company strategy and the harmonisation of individual behaviour with collective culture.*
- *A strong interactive component* among participants in the form of simulation exercises.
- *A personal development aspect* – however, not with the intensity of a counselling course. It is a fine line.

In addition, the program should feature:

- *A minimum of two instructors* with a strong, relevant and complementary background. I cannot emphasise this enough. A successful businessperson with no coaching background or a highly acclaimed clinician who knows nothing about business are not, in my opinion, suitable staff choices.
- *A rigorous assessment methodology,* based on the trainee's presence and contribution, a practice placement, which should ideally be presented to the rest of the participants, and optionally a thesis. I personally also believe in integrating some kind of examination covering the taught material and core reading list; however, I have received a lot of criticism for this, primarily from good friends and colleagues.

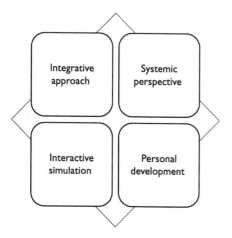

Figure 1.2 Coaching training content

- *High recruitment standards*, in terms of the candidates' experience, expertise, qualifications, relational abilities, emotional intelligence and level of personal maturity.
- *Some kind of recognition or accreditation from an organisation such as the International Coach Federation (ICF), the European Mentoring and Coaching Council (EMCC), the Association for Coaching or similar.*
- *A strong reputation* and references deriving from past alumni would be an added bonus.

The above are, in my opinion, the absolute minimum prerequisites of a decent training, and as a member of the Accreditation Assessors of the Association for Coaching, I have worked hard towards their implementation.

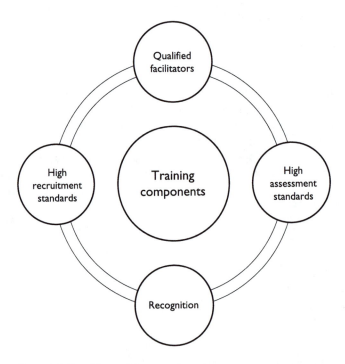

Figure 1.3 Coaching training components

Chapter 2

Coaching methodology

I can still clearly recall my first day as a psychotherapy post-graduate student. Upon being invited to express my expectations of the training, I immediately presented my desire to acquire the necessary "methodology" and get out there and *make* people live better lives. By the time I attended my coaching training, several years later, I knew better than that. I had come to realise that tools are only as good as the professional using them. However, I had also come to realise that methodological aspects, such as structure, boundaries and professional arrangements are an essential cornerstone (as indicated in Figure 2.1) for good practice. Therefore, this chapter (as well as Chapter 9: Coaching for impact) is dedicated to exploring the application of theory in a way that will support your practice, before, during and after your actual coaching session. In other words, "sharpening the saw", before trying to cut the tree (Covey, 1989, p. 287).

During the earlier stages of our coaching career, we seek the models that hold the answers and try to hold on to them for dear life. In addition, we also hope that these models will be *linear*. So for some time, I hoped that the time frame and

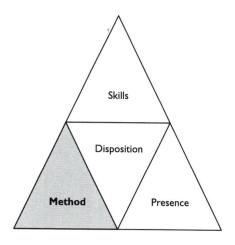

Figure 2.1 The coach: Method, an essential cornerstone

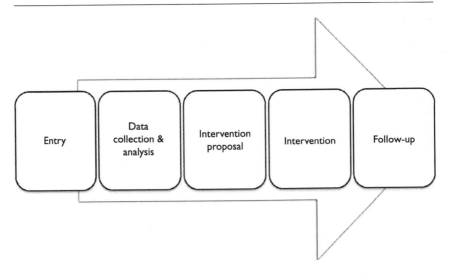

Figure 2.2 Impact 5 Stages

order of a coaching engagement could be depicted through Figure 2.2 , which I proudly named "Impact 5 Stages" and even went on to share with my students and trainees for a while.

It was not – too – long before I realised that in practice, the above sequence is a practical impossibility. Even though I have kept the basic diagram in my proposals to companies for the sake of simplicity, the fact remains that the three stages in the middle take place throughout the engagement and in any given order (not to mention the fact that, for example, *Entry* often creates room for *Data collection* and *Follow-up* is part of the *Intervention*, to name but two further nonconformities). In addition, the sequence is uncontained and isolated and lacks the fundamental element of the consultant being supported by aspects such as *supervision* and *boundaries*. The result was Figure 2.3. When reading this chapter, taking the time to compare and understand the differences between Figure 2.2 and Figure 2.3 may prove extremely helpful in achieving an understanding of the cyclical nature of coaching; and in providing you with a head start, which I also wish I had had at the beginning of my career, despite the fact that certain things are best learned rather than taught.

It is worth noting that both models, "Impact 5 Stages" and "Impact Coaching Cycle" are as relevant for executive coaching as they are for *Organisational Development*. Whenever possible, given that this book focuses on the former, I will highlight the inexorable links between the two disciplines.

Entry

Entry is the term coined to describe the period between the initial contact with the client and the moment your remuneration (provided it is not a pro-bono

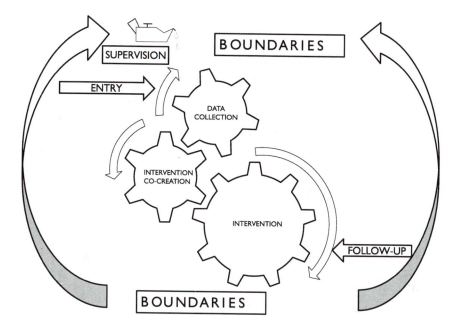

Figure 2.3 Impact Coaching Cycle

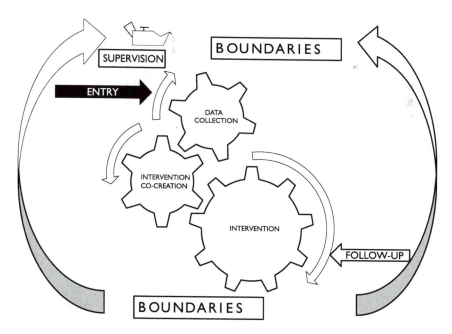

Figure 2.4 Impact Coaching Cycle: Entry

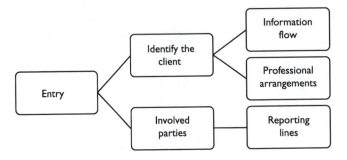

Figure 2.5 Entry considerations

engagement) for your services begins. This may sometimes include an initial unpaid meeting with the executive (sometimes called a "chemistry" or "fit" meeting). The clarity, transparency, expectations, deliverables and future collaboration parameters that will be established during this stage cannot "make" our success; they can, however, "break" it. I have therefore opted to present its components with a fair amount of detail. Figure 2.5 outlines some key considerations:

Initial meeting

The initial meeting ought to be an indication of what will follow and provide the human resources (HR) executive or other sponsor (or the coachee in the event of a chemistry meeting) with an authentic sense of who you are. If you are an empathic, emotionally intelligent consultant originating from a psychotherapy background, perhaps, there is no point in putting on the hat of the hard-nosed businessperson who always goes for the kill (and vice versa). It is important that you are able to *support what you will be doing with who you are.* Even though achieving balance and versatility helps, it is most likely that you will be more of one thing and less of another. Honour that. Trying to guess the client's preferred profile in order to adjust by wearing your chameleon suit or pretending to be a jack of all trades will jeopardise the sustainability of your intervention, and even if you do manage to get the job, a poor fit may mean a blow for your reputation; and *there is not one single contract that could be worth that.*

Identifying the client

It is, of course, very clear for whom the coach works – for the client. However, who is the client? For some of you, it may be obvious: the coachee, of course. I wish to question this notion. In the case of self-funded private clients such as small business owners, entrepreneurs, etc., it is clear that you and your client are ready to take on the world for their interest and their interest alone. However, when a corporation wishing to develop their executive funds the engagement, it is clear that there is more than one stakeholder. If one wanted to, one could even go as far as stating that since it is the corporation that pays the bill, the focus regarding the generation of added value should be primarily (if not solely) on the company and the alignment of the coachee's performance with the collective strategy and mission. The easy way out of this practical and ethical dilemma is to assume that what is good for the coachee cannot possibly be bad for the company. I can guarantee that you will come across cases (not very often, it is hoped) whereby this is not the case.

Case study 1: The IT expert

The coachee, a highly skilled and specialised IT expert, has been working for a large multinational in the Food and Beverage industry for the past 6 years, with a wage well below the industry average and very little scope for moving to a higher position. She is heading a rather small IT department and her career advancement possibilities are compromised and hindered, especially since rotation is not an option. She has little perception of the market circumstances and opportunities that surround her, and all the company wants from me is to provide a few sessions to support her time-management and delegation skills. To make matters worse, I am at the same time contracted by a leading technology firm and well aware that they would pay a pretty penny for her services.

Is my role to support the coachee's advancement or ensure that the company gets what they asked for?

Now consider the contrasting implications (or rather lack of them) that apply in the event that the executive had hired me privately.

In your daily practice, it is difficult to stick to strict principles. In theory, the fact that the organisation funds the engagement ought to mean that the coach's loyalty and allegiance lie exclusively with them; and that your primary goal is to *align the executive's performance with the organisational strategy*, since after all, you are an Organisational Development Consultant, featuring strong executive coaching expertise. In practice, a clear-cut distinction is very difficult. After working with someone for several months towards their development and having watched them grow and evolve, it is hard to keep your personal feelings and allegiance away from your professional Persona. After all, your job is to maximise potential. Keeping the engagement's sponsor (usually the HR Manager) in the loop with *transparency* helps matters a lot. In addition to being a support, both for you and the coachee, and a welcome calibrating factor, it also helps the consultant to maintain clarity with regard to who is paying the bill and, to an extent, who should mostly benefit. It is to be hoped that the interest of the coachee and their organisation will be mutual and thankfully, it usually is. However, the above considerations will help you manage risks, internal and external, if and when needed. I consider the issue of understanding who our client is to be vitally important. As far as I am concerned, it is practically an ethical issue. Recently coaches have taken to calling the party who pays the "sponsor" and calling the coachee the "client". I feel this is neither here nor there. You will at some point be required to make a decision with regard to whether the client is the paying party or the coachee.

Information flow

As indicated in the Introduction, access to information is a primary aspect in securing influence – the other two being access to resources and managing relations. At the same time, *managing information flow* is a prerequisite for securing optimum circumstances for coaching. The sub-section that follows, "Contracting", explores the issue of confidentiality. One of the best ways to safeguard it is to have your coachee write up their own progress report. They should also ideally be present in meetings that concern them. We don't, however, live in a perfect world. Even though coaching does not contain a direct component of assessment (and this should be made clear at the beginning as well as in all relevant communication, cover letters, etc.), you will from time to time find yourself face to face with the CEO, the line manager or the HR Director and you will be invited to "share your opinion about the executive, their potential and capabilities". What is vital at this point is not to disclose any of the session's content. This would be a breach of trust and, in my opinion, it also dents your credibility in the eyes of the "interrogators". Working your way through a negotiation with your coachee, regarding what they are comfortable with you sharing, in advance, may be the way forward. The seasoned consultant may even take this opportunity to support their coachee (as well as the company) by acting as a "bridge" that will strengthen the relation between the two sides and help them understand each other better. This approach, however, entails risks and should be avoided unless you feel great confidence in the outcome. It is best to respond with a general process-related comment (e.g., "we are tackling challenges at an appropriate pace") and if things get "too hot", indicate that you are not at liberty to share more. If boundaries have been well set at the beginning and your contract covers you (as explained below), this should take care of things.

Case study 2: The directive CEO

The coachee is a top-level executive in his early 40s with a leading regional role and has been on the fast track for the past 5 years. His progress has, in some ways naturally, come to a stop, since the next likely position would be that of CEO. I have been recruited to coach most of the Senior Management Team and even though HR has provided me with ample support and background, there is no real agenda or direction. The CEO gets involved at the end, effectively in order to hear my assessment about his team members. In the case of this particular executive, there is bilateral tension, since the newly appointed CEO is unlikely to be going anywhere for some time and my coachee feels that his wings are clipped in his current position. I am the recipient of ample information (mostly emotional) from "both sides" and it is possible that the relation is not sustainable. The request from both sides is fairly simple: The CEO wants my coachee to take a step back and stop being antagonistic, demanding and provocative; my coachee wants guarantees that he is next in line to become CEO. I am being invited to manage systemic conflict as well as act as a communications bridge between the two men. I opt for transparency and upon sharing some of my concerns with the Head of HR, I find myself in the CEO's office, for our customary wrap up (which comes at the end of six sessions). During the meeting, I make an attempt to address systemic issues and identify if there is some way that my coachee could in part get what he wants (such as a change in job title that would provide him with the sense of recognition he needs and "buy" the company some time, whilst keeping a competent team member on board). Despite being treated with respect, it is clear that the expectation is that I will not work with the relation between the company and the coachee, but with the coachee alone (perhaps by "convincing" him that he should be happy with what he has already).

In part, the limitation was that I had been hired as a coach rather than as an Organisational Development Consultant. In part, perhaps, there was no solution to the problem and I executed my task precisely as the system led me to. What's certain is that challenges such as information flow, transparency and acting as a messenger, from the coach's part, require copious attention and at times, you will find yourself in compromised, lose–lose positions. Growing smart and experienced is the best you can hope for.

My coachee left the company a year later, having secured a hefty package; the CEO is still in place, a good 5 years later, as is the HR Manager. Despite receiving plenty of training contracts from the company, I was not again invited back to coach (though I have little way of knowing if coaching programs were repeated).

At this point, it is also worth pointing out that information should flow both ways; therefore you may wish to have access to data concerning your coachee (past assessments, internal rotation, aptitude and personality tests, etc.). I personally do not find this information very useful and I rely more on other data generation and collection approaches, which will be extensively covered in Chapter 4 (Fundamental skills). However, some coaches, especially those originally from an HR background, may need it and make excellent use of it to form a spherical picture.

Contracting

There is a wealth of sample consulting and even coaching contracts that you can pick up on the Internet. If you are confident and experienced in drafting contracts, you may wish to skip this part. However, there are a couple of tips and areas for consideration, which could save you a lot of trouble; I wish someone had pointed them out to me a decade or so ago.

More often than not, the client will deliver a pre-made service provider agreement, which you will, it is hoped, be permitted to amend. At the same time, you may be required to produce your own (especially when working for private clients as opposed to corporations), and it is important that the agreement creates the circumstances that will enable you to work to the best of your ability. Issues that ought to be addressed in a contract are the following:

1 *Project scope and purpose:* This may range from specific deliverables (such as time-management skills, delegation skills, negotiation skills, etc.) to a much broader description ("executive coaching sessions"), or may even be subject to a Needs Assessment diagnostic procedure. Such procedures (e.g., 360-degree surveys) could be mentioned separately under a heading "Subject of agreement/ services".
2 *Timeline:* This section marks the beginning and end of the engagement and the billable hours, including the time you will be spending on activities such as drafting reports and analysing findings that take place beyond the face-to-face context.
3 *Location.* Sessions may take place at your premises or the client's, depending on what's mutually convenient.
4 *Client obligations:* This includes agreeing access to data, allocating an administrative contact from the client's side and anything else you deem necessary.
5 *Remuneration:* Your hourly or daily rate and payment terms go here.
6 *Termination:* Things don't always go as we plan. If for any reason, the agreed engagement does not complete (especially if you offer your sessions in clusters, like I do), you may choose still to be paid for all or part of the engagement. It's an individual choice.
7 *Cancellation policy:* In my opinion, this is one of the most important and overlooked aspects of a coaching engagement. A change or two when it comes to prescheduled sessions may not seem like the end of the world, especially if it is due to misfortune or inevitable difficulty from the client's side. However, not incorporating a cancellation policy may result in a lose–lose situation that stems even beyond missed income. My psychotherapy background dictates that all missed sessions are charged for. There are a variety of reasons, some which apply and some which do not apply for coaching. Whatever the case, you will need to decide for yourself what works best and what you feel is fair for both sides (for example, a 7-day notice policy); but whatever you do, do not ignore this issue. I personally charge if a *scheduled* session is missed or cancelled. This way, I do not have to carry a burden which is part of the

client's responsibility, or experience any resentment or frustration, which may somehow find its way into the work, for lost income and time.

8 *Expenses:* If travel and accommodation result in significant expenses, you may wish to secure compensation.

9 *Confidentiality:* If harm to self or others is not disclosed by the client, then the *content* of the sessions ought to be confidential. One of the ways that you may wish to tackle this, especially since supervising officers may want to receive a written progress report, is to request that the coachee writes this. This approach entails several benefits such as encouraging the coachee to reflect on and identify their progress and gains; it establishes transparent flow of information and it is time-efficient for the coach. I cannot recommend it enough.

10 *Copyright:* Your material is your own and especially if you have invested hours of research and development to produce it (let's not forget that many coaches are also trainers), you will want to protect it.

11 *Code of Ethics:* Your accrediting body or the body in which your firm is an organisational member (if you work within a consulting firm) should be able to provide a Code of Ethics. The Association for Coaching (AC), International Coaching Federation (ICF) and European Mentoring and Coaching Council (EMCC) are three such organisations. In recent times, (2016), the AC and the EMCC have been engaged in publishing a common Code of Ethics, which will, it is hoped, soon become universal. It makes sense to have standardised procedures and guidelines when it comes to business.

12 *Arbitration:* As already indicated, not everything goes according to plan. Even though this requires a lot of good will from both parties once things go sour, it may still be possible to avoid costly legal battles by appointing the appropriate, mutually acceptable arbitrator. Supervisors may at times be useful in this context.

Issues surrounding the parameters and boundaries of a healthy, mutually beneficial collaboration, within or beyond contractual agreements, will appear throughout the book.

Involved parties

Inviting and securing the involvement of key players when coaching, particularly when not self-funded, is fundamental; especially if you are keen on securing long-term benefit for the organisation rather than short-term benefit for the coachee. There are up to six key players in a coaching engagement serving a different purpose, and at least three (and up to five) of them should be present at the kick-off meeting:

1 *The coachee:* Obviously this is the central figure and their development (primarily in relation with the company's well-being, but also autonomously) is the priority.

2   *The coach:* This brings the list of the two "usual suspects" to a close.

3   *The HR department:* This is usually the coordinating sponsor of the whole project and I always ensure they are made aware of their role as a *fellow consultant* in the project (this is why the Impact Coaching Cycle indicates intervention co-creation). Synergy, good will and coordination, safeguarding the contract, supporting appropriate information flow, safeguarding logistics and establishing a single point of contact are vital success prerequisites.

4   *The line manager:* The assumption is that the line manager (unless you are coaching the CEO) has worked alongside the coachee in nurturing a development plan, and in the event that the coachee is a high-potential candidate in the pipeline of succession planning (i.e., a candidate for replacing the line manager when the time is right, a rather frequent request), they are the person who can provide feedback; both with regard to what the position requires as well as what the coachee's focal points for development are. This is another useful ally and especially in the absence of HR, they may form the third pillar.

5   *The company CEO:* The head of the company should be in a position to provide general feedback and direction with regard to the company's mission, principles and expectations for its top talent for the future. They do not necessarily need to be present at the kick-off meeting; however, their being accessible to the coach can be a great asset.

6   *The coach's supervisor:* Receiving supervision is as useful to a human coach as a check-up and a service are to a mechanical one. Would you embark in a vehicle if you knew that no one had ever inspected it? We will explore supervision further at the end of this chapter.

Reporting lines

In the context of *reciprocity* alone, it is fair to provide some kind of progress report for the company: Your coachee benefits from the company's investment and you make a living because of it. As indicated, my position is that the coachee should write this report. However, who should be the recipient? Most of the time, the HR department is responsible for collecting those reports, especially if they have also acted as the sponsors of the whole project. They are also usually your administrative contact point, arranging appointments and securing the smooth flow of the whole process. Sometimes, it may be the executive's line manager and from time to time even the CEO. It is not your job to decide who will receive the final progress report; it is, however, your job to obtain this knowledge at the very beginning, so as to make sure that the intended recipient is present at the kick-off meeting, in order to provide their feedback as well as support you and the executive in prioritising objectives and deliverables. Establishing reporting lines in a transparent way is not just a good way to support your coachee's progress; it is also vital in managing your own time and resources. For example, if you have to go to the company three or four times outside the contracted engagement sessions in order to inform the HR department, the CEO, the line manager, the

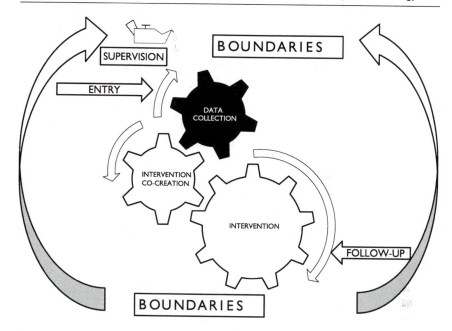

Figure 2.6 Impact Coaching Cycle: Data collection

Regional Director, etc., about your work with the coachee, this may be something you want to be aware of, before presenting your quote per coaching session and your hourly rate.

Data collection

As you can see, the middle section of Figure 2.6 is presented as mobile and interdependent. This is because the three stages presented (data collection, intervention co-creation and intervention) can and usually do take place simultaneously. The consultant is always collecting relevant data, which generates ideas (another continuous process), which ends up in intervention (which may generate more data, which may trigger more ideas and so on and so forth . . .). However, let's postulate that there is a starting point and take things from there:

The importance of *collecting data* in executive coaching, before co-creating a proposal with your client (to be explored in the very next section), is fundamental. In addition to the information made available during the first meeting with the HR department or the executive's line manager, you may also choose to increase your chances of delivering a focused intervention by also collecting the following data:

- past assessments and/or performance appraisals;
- the executive's role rotation over the years;
- profiler results (Myers–Briggs Type Indicator [MBTI], etc.);

- brief discussions with some of the executive's colleagues (obviously with the coachee's consent);
- information about the executive's company such as vision, mission, principles and other aspects that the executive's performance should be aligned with.

It is advisable to restrict the above to a minimum, since once the actual coaching begins, there will be ample opportunity to explore matters further by *generating data*, which is a different aspect of the work altogether and will be explored at length in Chapter 4: Fundamental skills: "Generating data".

Data collection plays an even more important role when coaching a group of executives whom you will also have the opportunity to train via a workshop. Such an arrangement gives you the opportunity to work with and within a system, which is no negligible advantage.

Intervention co-creation

Coaching greatly differentiates itself from training and even mentoring in that it is synergistic and promotes mutual responsibility. As I always tell my coachees, *your input in this process will match the output*. The same goes for when you are preparing to submit a proposal with your thoughts and ideas. The work needs to integrate several of the aspects that the company has shared and made available to you during the initial contact, concerning primarily the needs they want to

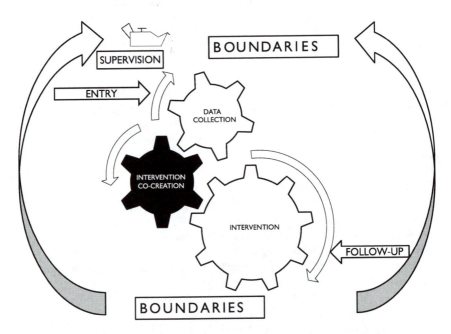

Figure 2.7 Impact Coaching Cycle: Intervention co-creation

address with your help. In that respect, *your intervention is co-created* with the help of the company. Even though you should allow for some flexibility, the fundamental aspects of what you will be doing should be clarified in a *proposal*, and nine times out of ten, companies will require one. The proposal also needs to showcase your practice and achievements. Finally, it should clearly indicate how your expertise and experience match the company's and the executive's agenda. Below I outline the headings you may wish to consider including in your proposal:

- *The scope and purpose of the intervention:* This indicates the number of participants, the overall aim of the project and additional services it may entail (executive coaching is often part of an Organisational Development intervention and may also contain training modules).
- *Who you are:* This may entail a brief history of your practice or organisation as well as your mission and vision.
- *Your services:* In addition to executive coaching, you may offer training, consulting or even corporate counselling if you originate from a psychology background.
- *Your methodology:* As indicated, "Impact 5 Stages" (Figure 2.2) is a comprehensive enough model. You may wish to create your own, as I have (effectively the one we are currently covering in this text).
- *Your client list.*
- *The parameters of collaboration between you and the company/executive:* This is the part that you need to write from scratch each time. It presents timetables and goals, mentions the tools you may need to use (such as customised 360-degree surveys, which we will be exploring in Chapter 4) and overall, needs to convey that *you intend to intervene in a way that matches and meets the company's needs rather than in a way that outfits your knowledge.*
- *Professional arrangements:* Your rates, the location, cancellation policies and perhaps terms of payment (effectively a summary of your contract as presented in the sub-section under "Entry").
- *References:* People or companies that your client can contact to find out what an excellent job you have done. Ideally this should be your whole clientele as presented in your client list.

Intervention

The intervention is the actual work and it makes sense to highlight the parameters and boundaries that surround the delivery of your service.

Number of sessions and frequency

My first advice to you is to offer your sessions in clusters. *How many sessions should each cluster include, though*? Too few, and you will not have a chance to

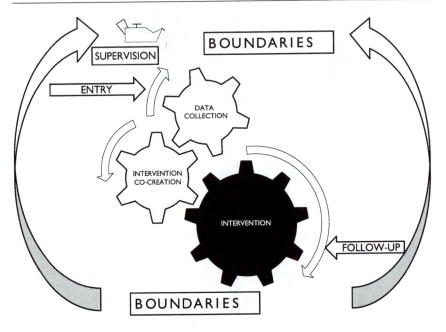

Figure 2.8 Impact Coaching Cycle: Intervention

produce results. Too many, and you may end up dragging on a collaboration that is not producing optimum results for longer than you ought to. I opt for clusters of six. I find that this gives me and the coachee a fair shot at creating awareness and momentum, and if things are working out nicely between us, we may opt to renew for a further six as many times as we choose to. Opting to interrupt the engagement may be due to lack of results as well as the fact that you have covered the ground you needed to cover. I also opt for a few weeks' break between the fifth and sixth session to give my coachee a chance to put into practice our gains, and a few months' break between each cluster of six. My preferred *frequency* for the rest of the sessions is a minimum of 1 week and a maximum of 3 weeks in between, depending on what the coachee has to achieve and the support I perceive they need. Following the end of the contracted engagement, a follow-up every month in the beginning, and every few months as time goes by, can work miracles in terms of rendering progress sustainable or making sure that new challenges are met with support and the right conditions for evolution to continue.

Needless to say, this needs to be contractually agreed and remunerated. There is a difference between being available for your coachee, once the engagement is over, for a quick phone call or email, and offering them a monthly follow-up meeting for free for the next 2 years. Unless it is a pro-bono engagement, this is usually a result of inexperience, desperation, a tendency to compensate for having conducted poor work, insecurity, low work volume and other aspects that constitute *very* poor practice.

Duration of sessions

The second consideration when conducting coaching is the *duration* of the session. With a background in psychotherapy, I prefer to avoid the "50-minute hour" (a term coined to describe psychoanalytic sessions, which last 50 minutes) and go for 45 minutes. Some people feel this is not enough. I personally like the mild sense of urgency this generates and find that it supports the maintenance of engagement for both parties. Energy levels tend to drop as time goes by. It is also worth sticking to your boundaries. Providing more than you have agreed, and been contracted to, diminishes the value of your service, both for you and your client. It also shows a lack of control and an anxiety to compensate for the quality of your service with the quantity of your service. Overall, I consider it very poor form and destructive modelling. Don't do it.

Billing

The 45-minute hour is very convenient in terms of billing. In the rare event that your client needs a "double" session, then you can provide it at double the rate and still work, marginally, within a time frame that is not exhaustively long. It is worth adding that I rarely provide double sessions, and when I do, I want to make sure that it is not a request based on anxiety and need. This creates a frame of dependency, an inclination to be an "anxiety alleviator" and a direction of "troubleshooting". Coaching is a paced, proactive, strategic procedure. You need to model this sense of "calmness" and "control" to your coachee by what you do and who you are. Don't fall into the trap of being a *saviour* or even a *rescuer*.

Follow-up

Most interventions (tin-can training programs, in particular) are eventually a flop primarily for a single reason: They have not been designed to have sustainable impact. Most trainers, coaches, consultants, etc., can design and deliver an adequate intervention. It is, however, worth remembering that as a coach, you will not be there forever. You must therefore devise safety mechanisms which bolt the coaching impact in place.

The first method I use is to invite my coachees to keep their own process notes (as mentioned, this is also what we co-submit to the sponsor, be it the Head of HR or line manager). This ensures that long after I leave, a summary of our work, triggering and stimulating the achieved transformation, will be available.

The second method I use, whenever I am given the opportunity to coach a group of executives, is the creation of *peer-coaching couples*. We will expand on this aspect in Chapter 6: Systems-focused executive coaching: "Prerequisites and circumstances".

The final ace up my sleeve is *following up* my work. This means going back after a few months have gone by to check up on progress and provide any support

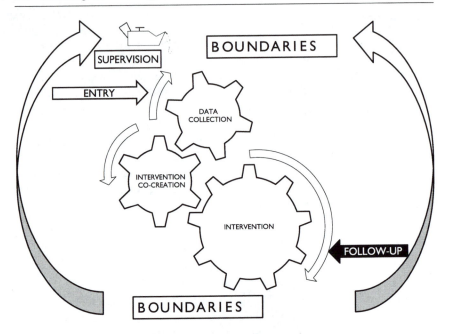

Figure 2.9 Impact Coaching Cycle: Follow-up

necessary. In order for this *calibration* to be effective, there needs to be some kind of *measurement*.

Endless pages have been occupied, presenting how the results of coaching can be measured. It is almost as if coaches feel they need to justify their existence through quantification alone. I have often been on the receiving end of this phenomenon, with the HR Director, almost bemused, asking me how I will measure the outcome of my intervention. The response to this entails several dimensions and I feel it is worth mentioning them, since progress assessment is essentially a part of follow-up.

The first and most obvious response is that *it is nigh impossible to attribute change or improvement to one single factor*. Even sales figures, in theory the most easily measured function, can be tricky to account for. Was it the brilliant marketing campaign? The new Sales Director? The training the sales force received? The new advertisement? The competition going bust? The increase in demand for one reason or another? The list – and the argument – can go on. Needless to say, this is not a good place to start your conversation with the HR Director. It is, however, vital to be aware of it, because it will support what will otherwise be an internalised defensive position.

The second dimension for measuring coaching progress has to do with the fact that the company's input is needed, if we are to know what needs to improve – and therefore be measured. As with everything else, *measurement will be co-created* and ideally agreed before the project begins. One company may require that the executive delegates more effectively and another that the executive takes more accountability. Or the same company may require different things from different executives. It is vital that these parameters are clarified at the kick-off meeting.

Third, it is indeed difficult to measure behavioural shifts. However, it is not impossible. Provided that the organisation has an adequate capacity for giving feedback, *you can administer a 360-degree survey at the beginning of the coaching process and then redistribute it at the end*. Therefore the changing impact that our coachee has on their associates can be used as the yardstick.

The final aspect that coaching should improve and which can perhaps be measured better than anything else is *speed*. As coaches, we aim to support our coachees in removing obstacles, such as limiting beliefs, counterproductive habits and isolation. Such intervention should result in improving speed and efficiency. Others should be able to notice this by being the recipients of a more proactive, confident and transparent communication, opening the way for a mutually benefi-cial collaboration. Identify tasks from your coachee's daily routine, especially those including the involvement of others and observe how their increased influ-ence minimises delivery time (fairly easy to measure) and maximises quality (somewhat more complicated).

Supervision

The oil-dispensing pump (painstakingly hand designed, may I proudly add, incorporating the full capacity of my limited graphic design skills) that I have

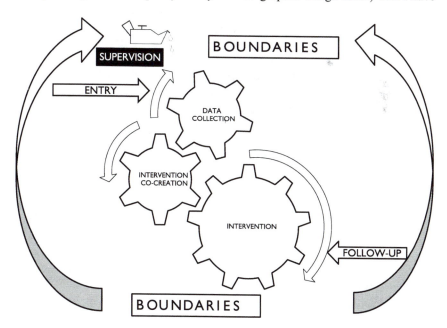

Figure 2.10 Impact Coaching Cycle: Supervision

incorporated into the diagram is *supervision*. Those of you partly familiar with internal combustion engines (such as automobile engines) will be aware that adding and changing oil is a vital component in ensuring that mobile, interactive parts can withstand the force, friction and pressure created within. The coaching relation is in many ways an internal process, since it is contained within several boundaries (confidentiality, time parameters, location, etc.). It is also a very interactive process, with several "components", such as the coach, the coachee, the market, the company and more, coming into direct contact. It is inevitable that force and pressure will be present; and as such, appropriate support and facilitation should always be available. Supervision is this very facilitation.

The concept of supervision originates from the world of psychotherapy. It is the process of a more experienced practitioner providing consultation and support to a less experienced professional, and in my opinion, this is the true definition of *mentoring*. The reasons that render supervision a necessity are numerous, the most obvious being *maintaining **boundaries** through ethical practice*. At the same time, it is important to be able to benefit from a senior practitioner's experience and expertise, thus adding *more dimensions* to your practice and approach. Understanding the *systemic components* of the coaching relation, identifying the *parallel process* and *extracting process from content* are advanced skills that a supervisor can instil in a less experienced practitioner (there is more on these advanced concepts coming up in Chapter 4). Overall and in my experience, I feel it would be fair to say that your training will carry you all the way to the beginning of your coaching journey, and supervision will be your vehicle to explore matters from there on. Its importance cannot be overstated.

Peer supervision is also an option; however, it is preferred that the group has a similar level of experience and expertise, preferably numbering a few years at least. Finally, *group supervision* is an excellent alternative to individual supervision, offering the advantage of versatility, a multifarious environment, increased interaction and higher energy levels.

It goes without saying that the choice of supervisor is of the essence and in addition to their personal credentials and experience as a consultant, good rapport is also crucial. A balance between challenge and support is vital. After all, *your supervising relation will in many ways be a reflection of your coaching practice.* Invest in it wisely. The return will be very much worth it.

Finally, the most important of all supervisors is the *internal* one. The internal supervisor is characteristic of a *Reflective Practitioner*. The term, originally deriving from mental health professions and now well spread into business and other disciplines, refers to the ability to continuously learn, self-assess, take ownership and deliberately *look inside to gain insight*. Within this text, Chapter 5 (Transformational leadership), as well as several sections in Chapter 3 (Presence) and Chapter 4 (Fundamental skills), heavily focus on the consultant's disposition and the ways in which this can benefit our clients.

Boundaries

In my opinion, coaching is not and should not be a profession in itself. It is a frame of mind, a leadership (or management) approach, a philosophy, a supplementary skill for executives, consultants, politicians or anyone who wishes to lead change and evolution. Nonetheless, as is especially the case with incubating ideas, it needs context, boundaries, institutions, associations, rules and regulations and generally and publicly accepted and agreed-upon *ethical guidelines*. The beginning of this chapter contains a plethora of guidelines on how to go about navigating within appropriate boundaries, in sections such as "Entry", "Contracting", "Information flow", etc. It is, however, worth exploring the issue of ethics and boundaries further.

Coaching is not only a new arrival; it is also a hybrid, whose origins can be traced back to psychology, sport, philosophy, existentialism, business, spiritualism . . . the list goes on. This makes the need for clarity even more urgent. Technically, the first place to seek and find such clarity is the Codes of Ethics published by major international coaching associations (ICF, AC, EMCC, etc.) that we mentioned in "Contracting", in spite of most of the guidelines being open to interpretation. By joining these associations, you agree to adhere to the respective Code of Ethics (they do not differ greatly from each other; however, you may find the AC and EMCC shared Code of Ethics at: www.associationforcoaching. com/pages/about/code-ethics-good-practice).

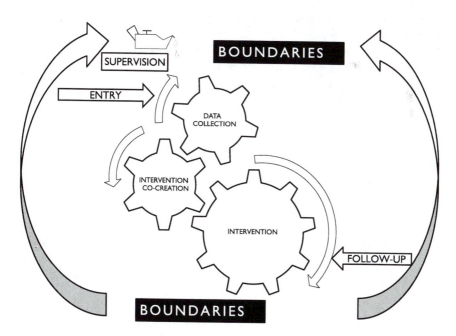

Figure 2.11 Impact Coaching Cycle: Boundaries

Admittedly, this is not a bad start and since these documents are readily and easily accessible, I do not wish to waste my reader's time or my book's space by reproducing them. There are, however, some considerations and dilemmas that are worth exploring and that have from time to time troubled me in my career as a coach. These dilemmas will greatly depend on context, your professional and personal background, your belief system and other factors. Below, I will focus on some of the most prominent ones, primarily based on my professional experience, taking for granted that:

- The coach is supervised.
- The coach is fit to practise.
- The coach engages in continuous professional development.
- The coach has received adequate and relevant training (as opposed to "hands-on", "life" or "field" experience).
- The coach works within their competency level and expertise (for example, refers to mental health practitioners if psychopathology is involved).
- The coach contractually addresses professional arrangements such as remuneration, cancellation policy, confidentiality, deliverables, reporting lines (please revisit earlier sections on "Entry" and "Contracting"), etc.

This text focuses on executive coaches offering their services to companies that wish to develop their employees. As far as I am concerned, it goes without saying that the former are recruited in the context of increasing the client's profitability or influence. Consequently, it is implied that *your client*, the party with whom you hold and honour a contractual agreement, is the company and not the executive with whom you have been assigned to work. Over the years, I have held debates on this matter with several people, many of whom have been my trainees, good colleagues and even friends. The issue of sponsors, a psychologically challenging and practically controversial topic, was not mentioned in any Code of Ethics until very recently. I was very pleased to observe that in 2016, in an effort to devise a single Code of Ethics by the Association for Coaching and the European Mentoring and Coaching Council, it was integrated.

Coaching is a profession that, more often than not, attracts people with a nurturing side, a humanistic and humanitarian mind-set (especially those coaches who originate from a mental health rather than a business background, or those coaches who reactively left the corporate world) and a certain romantic predisposition. Inevitably, it is very difficult for such people to accept that from time to time, what their job entails is actually to increase the profitability of an already large and profitable corporation. Therefore, they focus on the anthropocentric task of developing the person with whom they work.

For the most part, this is fine, since the coachee's evolution will directly benefit the company and this will therefore be a win–win all round. Things are not always this clear though, and it is the coach's task to understand the company's strategy and current needs and receive a relevant briefing, in order to align the coachee's performance and behaviour with that. Even though this is not usually the case, the coach's developmental priorities may differ from or even conflict with the company's strategic priorities (see sub-section on "Identifying the client"). In my opinion, deciding to prioritise the coachee's needs and wishes over the company's strategic needs borders on the unethical, and is more or less a breach of contract due to conflicting interests. I strongly recommend that coaches who are unable to manage this conflict limit themselves to working with private clients, whereby there is no question with regard to where their loyalties lie. Anyhow, in my experience, sooner or later these individuals honourably eject themselves from the system in the context of mutual dismissal, end up becoming "life coaches" or make the transition to other similar careers, such as "energy healers", which is much better than spending the rest of your working days consciously or subconsciously antagonising your client or feeling like you have "sold" your soul to the devil.

Finally, another consideration with ethical implications is the extent to which you can or should *socialise* with your clients. For those of us originating from a psychotherapy background, socialising with a client is an absolute no-no. Even self-disclosure is kept to a minimum or, in the case of strict psychoanalytic practitioners, absolutely forbidden. Coaching is not under any circumstances as absolute as psychotherapy and there are good reasons for this. On rare occasions, I have maintained a friendly relation with former coachees; and on even rarer occasions, I have embarked on coaching people with whom I have maintained a friendly relationship. Even though I do not view this as unethical, in the former case, the dynamic of caretaker and care receiver is difficult to overcome and therefore the reciprocity of the relation can be compromised, especially considering that the coach no longer gets paid. In the latter case, the aforementioned dynamic may enter the relation and upset the balance. There are two fundamental risks: that the coach is exploited (usually unintentionally) by the coachee; or that the coachee remains in a hierarchically lower position than the coach, which is not an ideal scenario for any relationship. Overall, it is better avoided than negotiated. Recently, Codes of Ethics have tackled this issue by indicating that any such relations should not take place during the engagement. This is ambiguous and open to interpretation; however, I am not sure if it can be clarified and contextualised any better.

Finally, and I have little wish to put my judgemental hat on, it is worth considering what your *social media* pages tell your clients about you. As far as I am concerned, attending to your public image is primarily an ethical obligation towards yourself and the profession/vocation you have chosen to serve.

Chapter 3

Presence

> Assess the quality of your relations; not by how snug they make you feel, but by how much risk they can survive.

A coach's *presence* will determine to a great extent the outcome of the coaching engagement and the establishment of *rapport* (to be examined later in this chapter). I have not yet concluded whether consulting (or anything else for that matter) is primarily natural talent and charisma or a result of hard work and commitment. The fact remains that presence develops over the years and in due time certainly falls into the category of unconscious competence. Nonetheless, it deserves a place of its own, separate from other coaching attributes, such as skills, which will be presented in Chapter 4.

Consequently, with regard to the issue of rapport, I am still in two minds as to whether it constitutes an ingredient of presence or if it is a skill that can be directly

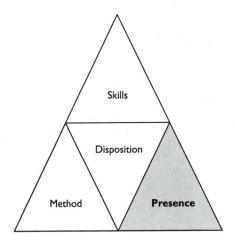

Figure 3.1 Presence

and methodologically taught. There is certainly an overlap and I have relocated rapport from Presence to Skills and vice versa (both in this book and in the courses I direct) several times. This process in itself is indicative of its multidimensional, fairly complex nature. Can a relational element be methodologically applied? For the purpose of this text, therefore, it will serve as a bridge that brings together Presence and Skills. Furthermore, I have opted to differentiate presence elements from coaching skills in the following ways:

1   Elements of presence, unlike skills, cannot be perfected through a structured, linear and orderly methodological approach (the likes of which will be presented in Chapters 4 and 9 that deal with skills).
2   Qualities of presence, unlike skills, are primarily dependent on experience and secondarily on expertise.
3   Presence develops primarily in an unconscious competence realm and secondarily in a conscious competence framework.
4   Presence elements are, primarily, reflexively at work. Skills are actively applied.

With the above in mind, let's go over the primary presence qualities that a consultant should aim to develop with time.

Positive regard and empathy: The Rogerian contribution

Energy saving tip: Pacify briefly instead of aggravating at length . . .

Carl Rogers, together with Gestalt's grandfather, Fritz Perls, dominated the psychology realm in the 1960s with their revolutionary ideas which brought about a schism from traditional Freudian approaches. Even though Gestalt has been integrated extensively into mainstream consulting and coaching (and will be explored throughout this text as well as with specific reference in Chapter 4: Fundamental skills), Roger's person-centred approach has played an equally important, albeit less "branded" role. Two of his theoretical positions, *positive regard* and *empathy*, can provide excellent support to coaches as well as therapists, especially during the early stages of their career.

Rogers used the term in his text "A theory of therapy, personality, and interpersonal relationships" (1959) and later expanded it in *On Becoming a Person* (1961): "The needs for *positive regard* and self-regard would never be at variance with organismic evaluation, and the individual would continue to be psychologically adjusted, and would be fully functioning" (1959, p. 224; emphasis added).

Without expanding further than necessary on psychotherapy jargon, we can deduce that Rogers advocates the creation of an environment and an approach that receives and treats people with acceptance and a nurturing disposition as opposed to judgement and prejudice. This would prohibit extensive focus on incongruence and maladjustment and would concentrate on the positives.

This is no doubt a noble position and positive psychology (a rather popular approach to coaching recently) has adopted it to a great extent. I would encourage anyone whose frame of mind is aligned with this attitude to adopt it, especially at the beginning of a coaching engagement. I am, however, also obliged to present my reservations, which are mostly a result of my own experience and approach rather than the objective truth.

My first concern is that business environments are, by default, antagonistic and speed of delivery is of the essence. To focus on supporting our clients, instead of challenging them, may be a good thing when dealing with damaged or troubled individuals. However, I feel that it may be borderline condescending, when working with a high-potential executive who wants to reach the next level of performance, yesterday.

My second objection is that putting yourself in a position to maintain a positive attitude, to practically like the person you are working with, can lead to numbing of your sensors and receptors. The fact that someone may cause us to experience negative feelings towards them (or the fact that we feel this way for our own reasons) constitutes valuable information and we may choose to utilise it as data and even provide it to our coachee as feedback. We will expand on this concept, the concept of transference and countertransference, considerably in Chapter 4: Fundamental skills: "Generating data".

The second Rogerian notion that executive coaches, especially those who are able to pick up the other person's energy and vibes, may be interested in is *empathy*. Empathy refers to the ability to tune ourselves in with the other person's experience and feel it as if it were our own. This alleviates the other's burden considerably, since they feel heard, understood and "together" (Rogers, 1975).

Clearly, an empathic coach has an advantage in forming a strong, secure bond with the coachee and the creation of rapport is very much facilitated. As previously, I invite the reader to consider two issues in relation to empathy: The first is that our ability to be empathic depends on a great number of factors and is directly linked with our history and capacity for caretaking. It is obvious that mothers will have an advantage in that respect, as will probably eldest children. If you do not have a natural capacity to be empathic, you will need to rely on your power of observation and data generation, in order to deductively or inductively discover where your client is "at" (a rather important piece of information not only in the long run, but also during each and every session).

On the other hand, if you suffer from being extremely empathic, again, there is a cost to pay. The first is that you pick up so much of your client's energy and burden that you end up carrying it for them. Supervision is a great way of addressing this challenge and your supervisor should be able to create circumstances for supporting yourself. The second risk for overly empathic coaches is that their identification with their client can sometimes cause them to presume things that are not actually there, purely based on their own personal experience.

It is not difficult to assess whether you are an empathic individual or not. Your body and its sensations (registering sadness, joy, fear, etc.) will inform you that you have picked up something which is not necessarily yours. This is called Empathic Attunement. Projective Identification is yet another strange form of empathy and we will explore it further in Chapter 4: Fundamental skills: "Generating data".

Authenticity

An important fact for the coach to keep in mind is that the coachee cares little about what we do. Our shiny tools and cutting-edge methodology do not account for much. They care even less about what we say. Memorising intelligent quotations that hold the secret to success from successful public or historical figures (or borrowing them from someone's Facebook status for that matter) will also not get us very far.

From the second we step into the consultation, our coachee will be watching very carefully to find out *who we are*. Even if they don't play "20 questions" with us and even if we don't catch their gaze looking for more than meets the eye, they will be looking to deduce whether who we are matches who we say we are and how we present. This is not necessarily a conscious process, nor does it necessarily result in a conscious exchange. It is therefore vital that the coach has undertaken the necessary personal work required, in order to feel fairly comfortable in their skin. Otherwise, the need to "inflate" our presence (or *Persona*) in order to "compensate" for what we feel we lack, will certainly bring about defiance, provocation and doubts from the client, who will rightfully question not just our authority, but also our *authenticity*. The polarity and bridge between the Persona and authenticity and how this is important for coaching will be explored in Chapter 5: Transformational leadership. It is, however, worth sharing a fairly standard definition of the term, as proposed by Block (2000):

> *Authentic behaviour with a client means you put into words what you are experiencing with the client as you work. This is the most powerful thing you can do to have the leverage you are looking for and to build client commitment.*
> (Block, 2000, p. 37)

The above definition implicitly makes reference to concepts such as transference and countertransference, empathic and sensory attunement, feedback and more. Chapter 4 (Fundamental skills) will explore these phenomena in more detail.

One of the most frequent ways of compensating is the heavy use of tools and the over-identification with a specific coaching approach. Of course, the trainee or beginner coach is very much entitled to use all the support they need. However, this "process" should have an expiry date and in due course, we should be able to develop our own, authentic, even idiosyncratic presence that is aligned with who we are. "Be true to yourself" might sound like a clichéd, "life-coaching" catchphrase; in this case, though, it is very pertinent.

Supporting yourself

The corporate environment is a cruel place. We abide by unwritten rules, which force us to tolerate and put up with hardship and pain: 15-hour days, missing lunch, endless meetings, fast-food meals, no breaks, sleepless nights, hunger, dehydration, exhaustion, constipation . . . the list goes on. The worst part is that we eventually become so desensitised that we mistake this existence for the norm. The executive coach has to do more than just prescribe the work–life balance recipe. They have to *model it*, by *supporting themselves*. As a coach, you should be able to create circumstances that enable the uninhibited utilisation of your potential. This ranges from the simple things, such as drinking a glass of water or getting up to gaze outside the window to refresh your perspective, to bigger things such as letting your client know . . . they have bored you to death (yes, this can be useful feedback too), or ceasing work with uncommitted or abusive individuals or companies who have recruited you to validate a self-fulfilling prophecy of failure.

Supporting yourself effectively is not only an issue of well-being and self-respect. It is also an excellent *diagnostic* and you should convey this to your coachees. If they are in a meeting that has gone on for 3 hours and they can no longer produce something useful, chances are everyone else is in the same position too; if they are so dehydrated that their headache is driving them through the roof, chances are they won't be able to finish that all-important report within the next 15 minutes; if they have not had a weekend break for the past 6 months, chances are their average day will be far less productive than it could be. A good way to identify executives who struggle to support themselves is to observe their *breathing*. Observe it and draw their attention to it, if it is shallow, infrequent or indicates anxiety. Needless to say, do the same with your own.

Putting up with and tolerating unpleasant circumstances is a false economy. Heroics belong in the battlefield and when there is no tomorrow. Coaching is about strategy. Support your coachee's investment in a sustainable future and the success of their company by encouraging them to look after themselves; and do that directly, through prescription, as well as indirectly, by modelling it through your very own presence.

Balance

Make people share by supporting them; make them reveal by challenging them.

Finding and modelling balance as an executive coach is vital. It provides a sense of stability and soberness for the client and renders the coaching sessions a safe place within which you and your coachee can take risks. We will refer to the concept of balance even more extensively in sections that follow, such as Chapter 5 (Transformational leadership), Chapter 6 (Systems-focused executive coaching) and Chapter 9 (Coaching for impact).

According to Nevis (1987, p. 126): "The aim is for the intervenor to be arousing but not unsettling."

For the time being, it is worth sharing some basic guidelines that can be applied in practice:

- *Balance pace:* The importance of managing *pace* cannot be overstated. If you try to do too much at once, the coaching structure may collapse. If you continuously miss opportunities to intervene and wait for the right moment too long, you will render yourself and your service irrelevant. Physical pace is also significant and we will explore it soon, under "Physical presence".
- *Balance (dis)position:* Our internal sense of balance will be revealed, no matter how well we think we can hide it. Anxiety to perform, fear of not being good enough, insecurity with regard to our skills, compensating by over-loading the session with technicalities and other internal liabilities will have a negative impact on the sessions. Try to sort out your "stuff" (for lack of a better word) to the best of your ability before undertaking to help others sort out theirs. Extreme *positions* are also best avoided or not expressed. We don't need to disclose everything to our coachee. The Persona (to be explored in Chapter 5: Transformational leadership) has its use. At the same time, being able to contain yourself when necessary is a sign of a balanced, expert practitioner. Finally, taking positions (whether your coachee's or that of someone else who features in your coachee's narrative) is usually an investment in future conflict and disappointment.
- *Balance frequency:* Unlike psychotherapy, sessions do not need to take place weekly. Balancing the *frequency* to match the desired outcome can be very facilitative. For example, if you have assigned a data collection or self-observation exercise, you may want to give your coachee a few weeks to progress. The same goes for the gap between the penultimate session and the final follow-up session. At the same time, you may choose to keep the frequency tight for the first few sessions to create rapport and generate some rhythm/pace.
- *Balance proximity:* With difficult, demanding and needy clients, the disposition is to either jump in and rescue them, perhaps by offering solutions, or jump out and evade contact, perhaps by relying exclusively on method. You should strike a balance by working right on the edge, right on the margin; by being available enough, yet *creatively indifferent*. In *Thus Spoke Zarathustra*, Nietzsche says (1961, p. 67): "I am a railing beside the stream; he, who can grasp me, let him grasp me! I am not, however, your crutch."

Suboptimisation

I have lost count of the occasions where I have had a heated debate with strategy consultants, usually over dinner or some other social occasion, with regard to the concept of *suboptimisation*. They advocate that it is an absolutely horrible thing and indicates below-standard performance. In some ways they are right, this is true. However, what Gestalt (and some systemic) theory disputes is that it may have its place. I will not resort to a guru's definition of the term, as it is, as far as I am concerned, rather straightforward: *input according to what the circumstances require rather than according to your optimum output.* To simplify this even more, think of driving a fast car in the rain, pedal to the medal, slick tyres fitted and without using the brakes. You get the picture?

Indeed, suboptimising our performance, output and energy does refer to under-delivering; not doing our best; not performing within the optimum. This may, however, be an extremely beneficial choice to make, both in relation to individual clients as well as teams. The reason is fairly straightforward: The client(s) will not necessarily benefit from what is our best, but will surely benefit from what is best for *them*. Being able to suppress our narcissistic urge to show how skilled, brilliant, eloquent or educated we are, in order to align our output with the client's capacity for input, is not just kind and noble; it is imperative.

Suboptimising and balancing are concepts that I have struggled with extensively when writing this text. As the book is intended to be as much a handy A to Z supplement for trainees as a stepping-stone for experienced practitioners, I have had to "accelerate and brake" on numerous occasions. This consideration should accompany the conscientious coaching practitioner at all times. If uncertain, ask your client if "they are with you", if "they are following you" or if "this works for them". You may be in for a surprise.

Physical presence

The way we present ourselves in the services industry is even more important than it is in retail and other markets. *We* are our product and some may argue that what you see is what you get. Dressing appropriately as well as authentically for each occasion is a good place to start. This means taking into consideration what we are comfortable in as well the nature of our client group. Dress codes will be different for an investment bank than for a start-up IT company, for example. And at the same time, and with the risk of stereotyping, a 60-year-old female coach who has been a humanistic psychotherapist all her life will probably get away with a vibrant, multi-coloured shirt more easily than the 45-year-old male coach who has been a C-level executive for the past 15 years.

Moving one step further from dress code, though, which can mostly be determined through common sense, I will provide a list of physical presence items we ought to address as executive coaches:

- *Language:* Our use of *language* needs to be characterised by balance. Even though our client is not very interested in coaching jargon, it is important that we are in command of consulting terminology. It is our code for communicating with colleagues and deepens our understanding of our craft. The person we work with (age, role, seniority, rapport) also determines our use of language. Taking too many liberties (such as using foul language or becoming overly casual) is best avoided. Finally, the language we use should represent what we stand for; otherwise it will come across as inauthentic and pretentious.

- *Body posture:* This will inevitably vary according to the content of our session. We will tend to adjust our *body posture* by moving in to pay closer attention to our coachee or lean back to give them space. I personally opt for the latter most of the time, and try not to signal what is happening for me to the coachee in a way that will condition them to produce what generates a "good" reaction or "interest" from my side. Not being too easy to read and allowing some anxiety to arise from the coachee's side because they can't adapt, please or control you is a powerful tool in the hands of the seasoned consultant. A coach should possess the power of deliberation and be in a position to monitor what they give out. This applies to body posture also. Observe it, practise it, test it, perfect it.

- *Rhythm:* In this instance, this refers primarily to monitoring speed, the speed with which you articulate and present information for a start. Identify cues which indicate that your client has reached capacity (or ask); use pauses effectively; support your delivery with your breathing and body posture; observe when anxiety forces you to speak faster than you would like to. It may sound Machiavellian and it probably is. A coach should be in a position to determine the *rhythm* of a coaching session, rather than allowing circumstances, fears or the client to drive them into working outside their supported performance zone. In the past, I used to consciously check in with myself to make sure that what was about to come out of my mouth was a well-supported, intentional, deliberate intervention that I would not regret making. In time, this became an unconscious competence. In recent years, I have allowed several minutes of fertile silence before responding to a client. Set the rhythm as well as you can. This will create a safe context for your client, who in their turn will aim to find ways of supporting themselves and their delivery, like you have.

- *Pace:* I differentiate between pace and rhythm in that *pace* is a phenomenon that has to do primarily with the totality of the work, and rhythm with each session separately. In that context, it is more difficult to observe in a non-abstract way and is less of a physical attribute. It is, however, something that you can *physically sense* and it refers to our body letting us know if the work is flowing well, or if the rhythm is irregular and interrupted. In that sense, our physique can diagnose good and poor rhythm for each session; and this information enables us to evaluate the overall pace. Frequent cancellations, rescheduled sessions, extensive small talk, poor follow-up and a sense of relief when the – endless – meeting comes to an end (probably mutual) are signs of poor rhythm during each session and consequently poor pace in the overall collaboration. An inconsistent, broken, interrupted, unnatural pace is a symptom that can signify a number of things (ranging from poor chemistry between the coach and the coachee, loose boundaries and lack of engagement to unaddressed or unfinished business, Projective Identification, etc.) and it is not to be ignored. To help differentiation even further, rhythm has more to do with the tactics in each session and pace has to do with the strategic totality of the work. Pace can include several different rhythms.

- *Energy* is a term often used in sports. In the context of executive coaching, it could be described as *the degree of engagement intensity*. For the coachee, this will for the most part be unintentional and fairly consistent according to their temperament and character. A coach, on the other hand, carries the responsibility of being in a position to monitor and partly control (not to the point of being deprived of all spontaneity) their energy levels. Suboptimisation, mentioned above, is possibly the ultimate tactic in monitoring energy levels. Being able to drop them slightly in order to contain the client's anxiety or tendency to panic and "overspend" themselves; adjusting them to support appropriate rhythm; donating some extra energy to mobilise your client: All are indications of a coach who can masterfully control and almost determine energy flow in the coaching session. The importance of such a skill cannot be overstated and the best way to develop it is to keep it within your awareness and to experiment with lifting and dropping energy until you can do so at will.

Rapport

All the presence elements previously mentioned (some of which will be presented below once again, this time in the context of rapport) play a crucial role in establishing *rapport*; that is, *in establishing a quality relation with your client that enables you to challenge and support them in equal measure*. The two aforementioned concepts (challenge and support) are key elements in working towards such an authentic relation.

In recent years, *rapport* has become a fashionable term. Even more so, since generating revenue became a bigger challenge and leadership started featuring as a meaningful business aspect. Rapport has been closely associated with empathy. According to Bluckert (2006, p. 31), empathy is about conveying and expressing something – a thoughtful, sensitive comment or a caring gesture. This is a perfectly acceptable aspect of rapport and carries echoes of Rogerian theory. Even though this is a beautiful thing, I find utilising *transference and countertransference* far more productive. Make a note of these terms, as we will be exploring and utilising them extensively in Chapter 4: Fundamental skills. For the time being, let's consider the *raison d'être* for relations, particularly in the business world.

The first thing that comes to mind is the quest for profit. However blunt it may sound, this does not stop it from being the truth. Companies and individuals recruit coaches in order to support behavioural aspects that will contribute towards the generation of profit. I feel it is important that this is more or less directly indicated at the beginning of the relation and that *common and mutually understood goals are established*. Therefore, I feel that the primary aspect in generating rapport in coaching, and perhaps in any relation for that matter, is *transparency*.

The secondary aspect is *clarity*. In coaching, clarity is promoted by establishing what is known as a *hygienic context*. Let's recall the first of two components of rapport: *support* and *challenge*. Reflect for a minute on what would make you feel supported as a client. The first thing, or one of the first things, would be a sense of *safety*. How is safety promoted? We mentioned the word "containment" earlier and it is worth mentioning again. Clients (regardless of industry and service provided) like to feel they are being "held". An excellent way to create a sense of holding containment for your client is to start by establishing *hygienic boundaries*. Funny as this may sound, insisting on applying and maintaining hygienic boundaries can make all the difference in the world. Such boundaries include the time, the place, the contract, agreed remuneration, commonly agreed goals and anything which will create the space and circumstances *to work on the job at hand rather than be constantly anxious about how rules of engagement and regulations are interpreted by both parties*. Boundaries support the coachee, the coach and, above all, the relation in equal measure. Never underestimate them.

Support, however, only accounts for getting half the job done – in my opinion, the easy half. The other half of the job, *challenge*, depends on your mastery of the *art of taking risks*. The primary risk one takes, as an executive coach, is to provide *feedback*. The secondary risk is to provide feedback that includes the coach's process as well; that is, letting the client know how their behaviour and presence make you feel in the "here and now" of the session, the impact they had on you over time, how you perceive them and relating this to how others may perceive them. Again, we will expand on the skill of giving feedback in Chapter 4. Needless to say, the coach's risk taking should act as an example for the coachee to open up and share with transparency and clarity. A compliant, pleasant, polite coach, serving clichés and working with standardised profilers, may win the popularity contest; however, it is unlikely that they will generate momentum for progress. Coaches should take risks. Anything else is simply avoidant or denotes inexperience. As always, we are invited to *lead by example* and to be rather than do or say. Risking a discrepancy in that department may be the biggest risk of all and one whereby the odds are against us. We have no other choice but to take it, should we wish to coach for impact.

Let's therefore present the actual steps that a coach should or could take in generating rapport. It is worth noting that the fact that rapport can be "prescribed" and "taught" renders it as much a skill as a presence element. Those in the know, though, understand that the latter is the prerequisite of a fruitful coaching relation.

1   *Disclose and share your process with your client:* Contrary to Roger's human-
    istic belief that unconditional positive regard should characterise the consult-
    ant's (therapist's) attitude towards the client, those amongst us who are more

psychoanalytically inclined, advocate that *the client should know how they are perceived.* For example, if their behaviour exasperates or distances us, then they should be made aware of that. It is very likely that this also happens to other people around them and, as such, this is an extremely valuable piece of information for them. (Or it could be a result of the chemistry of our relation, which, again, is worth exploring). We will expand on the issue of sharing feedback by disclosing our internal process to the client in the sections "Generating data" and "Giving and receiving feedback" in Chapter 4.

2   *Seek support from yourself and the environment:* Supporting yourself demands the creation of circumstances that transform your existence from bearable to comfortable. This may include drinking a glass of water, a toilet break, allowing for pauses at an appropriate time, regulating room temperature, finding a comfortable seat or position and many other aspects, which we often choose to tolerate rather than do something about. It may sound simple or even simplistic; however, the modern executive has been conditioned to withstand, put up with and endure near-unbearable circumstances. Requesting a break after staying put in a meeting for 3 hours is a risk worth taking. A coach who does not suffer from the same degree of desensitisation can deliver their services more effectively, whilst modelling self-support for the coachee.

3   *Give honest and clean feedback:* We will dedicate a whole section to feedback in the next few pages. However, in the context of supporting rapport in the coaching relation, it is worth mentioning that honesty is of the essence. You may choose to postpone giving feedback on difficult matters; however, do not fall into the trap of taking a position which you will be forced to alter in the near future. It renders you unreliable. Second, feedback needs to be clean; in other words, separate from assumptions and opinions (which do have a role to play, nonetheless). The risk of honesty usually pays a large dividend in the coaching relation.

4   *Suboptimise your energy:* Today's business environment demands that we maintain a high output at all times. Notwithstanding the risk of burnout that this entails, we also need to take into account a number of other factors. Our best is not always what is needed and we may need to adjust to the client's expertise, knowledge and energy levels in order to achieve the best possible result. Provide the client with what is optimum for them, not what is optimum for you.

5   *Promote a high challenge–high support ethic:* Before you take the aforementioned risks, assess how far you have come in creating common ground with your client. You may go as far as asking them what and how much they are able to withstand at a given time. If you get the feeling that the relation can contain the next level of challenge, then proceed further. Otherwise, play safe and patiently stand back for a while. As a rule of thumb – and this rings true for most relations – *the higher the quality of a relation, the bigger the risk it can survive.* The two are practically linearly correlated.

Chapter 4

Fundamental skills

This chapter started out its life under the title "Basic skills". As I drew out its skeletal structure, I realised that the title was misleading and misaligned with the rest of the book, which is an invitation to extend our practice beyond the basic. I therefore renamed it "Fundamental skills", and even though there is some mention of basic tools and "to dos", it is for the most part an invitation to take the risk of seeing beyond the obvious.

Our skill, as a coach, is the conscious, visible, overt contact point with our client. Even though, in my opinion, it is our *disposition* (Chapter 5: Transformational leadership) and *presence* (Chapter 3: Presence) that determine the dynamics and outcome of the coaching engagement, it is an indisputable fact that we cannot coach without skills. It is fortunate that, for the most part, these skills can be presented, almost taught in a practical, straightforward way.

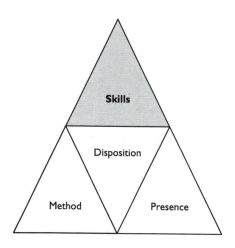

Figure 4.1 Skills

This chapter will therefore emphasise applied practice and focus on the following three skills:

1   Listening;
2   Generating data;
3   Giving and receiving feedback.

The seasoned consultant will keep in mind that presence and skill are interdependent and there will frequently be an overlap between the two. Rapport, for example, is a fine case where one could argue that it is as much an element of presence as it is a skill that can be learned and applied. Understandably, in the context of organising information for a textbook, some "grey areas" need to go into one chapter or another. This limitation need not apply in your daily coaching practice, and your client will care little if what you do falls into one category or another and even less about what it's called. For the time being, however, let's educate ourselves.

Listening

Whereas it may appear as the most straightforward of all skills, *listening* takes a long time and great effort to master. Most people listen with the intention of responding rather than understanding (Covey, 1989, p. 235: "Seek first to understand and then to be understood"). The good news is that this particular aspect of coaching can be approached with a fairly simple "do" and "don't" attitude, at least in the early stages. In addition to creating optimum circumstances for coaching, modelling good listening skills is an added, indirect benefit for the coachee.

Do use eye contact appropriately

Maintaining eye contact is one of the first myths we are obliged to dispel. Few things are more unsettling than a person staring at us at all times during conversation. Interruptions to eye contact, to provide our coachee with space to reflect and ourselves with space to contemplate (or support ourselves) can be very liberating. There is a reason why psychoanalysts sit behind their patients who lie down on the couch whilst free associating. Though I am not suggesting that we do that, feeling observed can act as an inhibition. Balance the (eye) contact between you and your coachee to support the lifting of self-consciousness and reticence. In due course, you should be able to regulate appropriate eye contact subconsciously and instinctively, by reading your client's body language and by recognising your own need for healthy withdrawal (there is more on withdrawal later in this chapter, under "The Gestalt Cycle").

Do paraphrase and summarise

One of the most useful interventions, when it comes to communicating (and this goes for all relations, not just the coaching one), is the use of the phrase, *"What I heard you saying was . . ."* and respectively, the question, *"What did you hear me saying?"* This approach does not only generate an excellent communication bridge; it also minimises the room for misunderstanding and aligns the two parties by bringing them onto the same page. It also aligns the coachee's communication intention with their impact and outcome. It's a coach's job to frequently inform their coachee of what their words and statements sound like and how they "come across". The primary benefit is that the coachee feels heard and attended to. The secondary by-benefit is that the coachee gets a fair idea of what others hear from them when they speak. The value of this intervention cannot be overstated. At the same time, the coach models the use of this technique for the coachee who can go out of the consultation and use it for their business (and personal) interactions to their benefit.

Do ask for clarification

This approach can either be genuine or a trick. If you have genuinely not understood what your client has said, it is important that you hear it again. This also strongly models the practice of not keeping silent when confused just because you are afraid those around you will consider you unwise. It also ensures that your client knows that you are paying attention to them and that what they are saying is important to you; so important that you must understand it. However, asking for clarification, or even going as far as pretending not to remember what was said, is also an excellent way to invite your clients to repeat themselves. This can be especially useful if what has been expressed has been unclear, confusing, senseless, imprudent, etc. and gives them the opportunity to "listen to themselves" one more time. I frequently employ this trick when I teach coaches too if I want to make sure they remember something important. You may choose to employ the trick or not, depending on how you feel about such approaches. Personally, I love them. However, do ask for clarification if you have not understood.

Display reflective patience

This is a virtue which comes with experience. In addition to creating space for your coachee, it also gives them a free run to provide you with information, which they may have otherwise not disclosed. A reflective, patient, non-judgemental presence can work wonders in giving permission for the coachee to move beyond their internal censor. It also provides space for the coaches to support themselves and withdraw to a space of *creative indifference.*

Do test assumptions

Making assumptions can be a great way forward in coaching, as long as you clearly indicate that what you are about to say is a result of deduction or simply an opinion. Again, this can be a way to let your client know how what they have said sounds (which can be useful feedback), or it can serve as a mild provocation (replace with instigation if you are not too happy with the term), which may trigger fruitful interaction. For instance, an executive who consistently blames others for their lack of success in their tasks, may benefit from hearing the coach say, "It sounds like you have very little control over your deliverables". Such statements can test your assumption, invite the coachee to review their situation or generate further dialogue. In any case, beginning your statement with, *"It sounds like . . ."* is an excellent coaching intervention.

Having looked at some fundamental guidelines for effective listening, it is worth going over a list of "no-nos".

Don't give uninvited advice

You are not an advisor, you are a consultant. Your job entails creating the circumstances for reflection and supporting your coachee's decision making. If you have answers for everything, not only do you arrest your coachee's individuation (we will explore the term "individuation" in Chapter 5: Transformational leadership), but you also jeopardise the benefits that the co-exploratory process can yield; and these are usually the most important gains in a coaching relationship.

Don't interrupt frequently

As indicated earlier, creating space is a prerequisite for a productive coaching session. This may include some silence, which you will be invited to endure. The coachee may be at a stage of *fertile void*. We need to be able to allow this. Experience will help you tune in and appreciate when to keep quiet.

Don't refer to similar cases of your own constantly

Let's face it. Things are not as strict in coaching as they are in psychotherapy, where self-disclosure is kept to an absolute minimum. From time to time, it may be useful to identify with your client and it may be welcome for your client to identify with you. Sharing some personal experience from time to time may help and I have often resorted to talking about my own experience, when it resembles my client's. However, this can't form the basis of your approach. Such frequent references will eventually stop you from listening to your coachee, since you will presume that their case is similar to yours; and that is the point where you start hearing what you want to hear or think you hear rather than what is being said.

Don't overwhelm with multiple questions

Women may prove more resilient than their male counterparts and be able to get back to you when required to answer three or four consecutive questions; however, it is certain that both you and your client will be spreading yourselves too thin. Not only will you jeopardise focus and create a sense of chaos and anxiety, but you are also running the risk of stimulating feelings of inadequacy in your client, for not being able to respond in a satisfactory fashion.

Don't rush into conclusions or solutions

Even though it is certainly useful to generate momentum for action, doing it too fast will simply render you a troubleshooter; and even if your coachee goes out there and delivers the solution as co-created, you will have missed the opportunity to *listen to what is troubling them rather than what the problem is.*

Generating data

The art of *generating data* for executive coaching is so important, it probably deserves its own chapter. Actually, it deserves its own book and this may be an idea for the future. For the time being, however, it belongs right here with the other two fundamental coaching skills. For a start, it is important to distinguish it from "Data collection" as presented in Chapter 2. During data collection, we gather information that is already available in one way or another and is for the most part recorded somewhere. Data generation is a whole different ball game. *The data become available because of the action we take to reveal it.* The data can therefore be open to interpretation and dispute; and as such, far more beneficial in the coaching process, since it entails taking the risk to present the data and relating well enough to take that risk. For the time being, it should suffice to underline that the actual *process* of generating data is probably just as important as the data it helps to generate; *for it provides an excellent pretext for contact.* The Diploma class of 2016/2017, upon observing me, decided to call this process *"Any Excuse"*; meaning that *any* action will generate a reaction and therefore provide opportunity for observation and relation.

Tools: The customised 360-degree survey

Profilers, tests and data-collection tools have been around for a very long time. They served a purpose in military recruitment (such as the pre-World War II MMPI [Minnesota Multiphasic Personality Inventory], which I remember administering in the early 1990s during my military service as a psychologist) or forensics to predict criminal behaviour. The most popular and widely used "profiler" for business and coaching is the *MBTI* (Myers–Briggs Type Indicator), which separates participants into 16 categories. There are also other profilers such as the *Belbin* and the *Enneagram*. They have all become increasingly popular recently, mainly because they have become widely available (and therefore do not require extensive training), and they can support beginner coaches to generate some seemingly intelligent content.

We will not be exploring the use of tests and standardised tools in this book. It is very easy to find out more about them through specialised publications or even the Internet. It is also fairly easy to obtain and administer some basic versions for free. The same goes for typical coaching questions ("powerful questions" as some like to call them). Even though they can be useful supplements and trigger food for thought, training in administering assessment tests without specialised coaching training does not suffice to deliver coaching interventions. Hiding behind technical, automated methodology to *compensate* for general anxiety, lack of experience and training and fear of lack of content is not recommended either. As time goes by and your know-how and expertise increase, you should be able to design *customised data generation/collection tools* and, most importantly, *use yourself* as a receiver for the client's transmissions.

Supporting our client's self-awareness is essential in developing their leadership profile: Executives and leaders should have a fair understanding regarding the impact they have on others. Collecting feedback (to be explored below) is a great place to start. Collecting feedback anonymously can be even better. An excellent way to achieve this is the use of *360-degree surveys*. A 360 survey is a questionnaire administered to an executive's manager, a colleague, a subordinate and an external associate (four directions providing a circular overview, accounting for the term "360 degrees"), inviting them to provide feedback on the "subject's" behaviour and/or performance. Several multinational companies make use of 360 surveys; however, they tend to eventually standardise them, which compromises the *focus* of the process on individuals. At the same time, there is usually wide scepticism regarding the *confidentiality* as well as *use* of the information provided; that is, they tend to be perceived as *assessment rather than feedback tools*. Finally, the use of language and overall format can be distancing and somewhat off-putting; and this is where a good coach's *tailor-made 360 survey* can come in and create ample opportunity for development. I would like to walk you through the development stages of a customised 360, since I feel it is in many ways superior to a standardised one. At the same time, co-developing a data-generation tool with your coachee adds several more dimensions to the work, such as shared accountability, opportunity to observe your coachee at work in real time, a sense of rapport deriving from a common goal and a lot more.

The first stage in utilising a 360, or any tool for that matter, is to identify areas that are of importance and consequence; both for the individual as well as for the company (if and when coaching is company-funded). There will, it is hoped, be an overlap. If you have undertaken to coach a group of executives, half or more of the questions can be the same for everyone and therefore with a focus on company-related performance topics; and the other half or less can be directly supplied by the coachees themselves. This is an excellent way to *engage the coachee* in the process, distribute accountability between you and promote joint ownership of the coaching progress.

Main headings can be decided either at a three-way meeting between the coachee, their supervisor or HR Manager (or project sponsor) and the coach in order to *invite the involvement and support of the main stakeholders*; or between you and your coachee during one of the first meetings. I usually request that development headings are limited to five. Such headings usually include influence, communication, motivation, leadership and other fairly broad and general traits and characteristics. It may be useful to be informed and guided by the company's mission and vision or even its strategy and current direction, especially if you are part of a restructuring process. In other words, you must keep the goals and objectives relevant to the company's needs. Remember that well if you wish to produce optimum results, gain appreciation as an agent of transformation and secure repeat business. Your success as a coach is not only assessed by your coachee; it is assessed by those benefiting from their progress and increased contribution to profitability as well.

Upon deciding on four or five headings that are important for the company's and the individual's progress, you need to identify behaviours and characteristics of the trait you are exploring. I usually suggest that three to five such sub-headings are adequate. After a certain point in your career, you will be able to generate such behavioural sub-headings at the blink of an eye; it is, however, important that you *step back and give others the chance to think things up for themselves* and try to primarily supervise and support rather than control and dictate the process.

Let's look at an example of how to set up your customised 360, by assuming that the company that has hired you considers influence to be one of its key values. Your first task is to work with your coachee in identifying the behaviours they consider relevant to influence. The process itself can prove to be an invaluable aspect of the coaching process, since you get to find out more about their belief system (Epistemology) and they get to challenge and explore what they stand for.

Below is a sample of what a segment of the customised 360 could look like:

Headings: (Traits, Values and Characteristics, usually around five): for example, Influence

Sub-headings: (Behaviours characterising the trait heading, usually three to five)

- I often turn to the executive for support, information and advice.
- The executive manages relations and alliances in a mutually beneficial way.
- The executive exhibits accountability for matters beyond their job description.

The respondents assign a numerical value, which indicates the degree to which they agree or disagree with each statement (Likert-type scale), thus rendering their job fairly straightforward and not demanding or time-consuming. I have experimented with tight scales of 1–5 and loose scales of 1–10, and usually I opt for a scale of 1–7. It is up to you and your coachee to discuss what suits the situation best.

The above process will produce approximately 15 questions (five headings x three sub-behaviours) that will assess specific traits directly related to organisational values. As mentioned, your coachee should get a chance to find out things about themselves directly; therefore, anything between one quarter and one half of the survey should be allocated to questions that they have devised in relation to things they want to find out about themselves. What I usually say to support the creation of this segment of the 360 is, "What would you be asking people about you, if for a minute they were forced to speak the truth and the truth alone?" There is no need for headings here and you may wish to let them experiment with open-ended questions, multiple choices, Yes or No responses and anything else they want to do (provided that you charge for the time you or your assistant devotes to analysing data). Over the past decade, some of the questions that have come up are as follow:

- The executive is the colour _____.
- The executive has a good sense of space.
- The executive does not lose their temper (too often).
- If the executive was an animal, they would be _____.
- The executive dresses appropriately depending on the occasion.
- What is the executive's main point for development?
- The executive walks the talk.
- The executive is punctual.

At this stage, you should encourage the coachee to freely explore issues they suspect they may need to improve on, topics they have little idea about, aspects they are curious to find out more about; and overall, establish a more liberal, playful, yet focused, direction. The benefits of securing this space for your coachee are numerous and invaluable.

Upon completing the survey design, you will need to aid your coachee in *identifying appropriate respondents*. 360s usually employ the help of a supervisor, someone who reports to your coachee, a colleague and an external person such as a client, an associate, etc. There are several considerations. Someone who does not know them well or long enough may not provide meaningful data; someone who has known them too long (say, more than 5 years) may generalise, usually in a positive way. You should also mention that there ought to be a balance in the mixture between people who tend to judge and people who tend to flatter. It is best to let them choose first and discuss their choice later, without necessarily amending anything. You may also choose to include more than four respondents, as long as the representation quota remains linear (i.e., two supervising managers, two colleagues, two reports and two external). The bigger the sample, the more reliability, validity and discrepancy issues will be identified and explored. For instance, if two of the people reporting to your coachee give completely different marks, or if supervisors mark very differently from colleagues, then this is worth exploring.

An option, which I frequently make use of (and which some people consider one of the four axes of the 360 instead of the external associate), is to invite the coachee to answer each question for themselves. The answers can refer to how they perceive themselves *or* to how they believe others perceive them. Inviting them to respond to both hypotheses may prove useful in exploring further discrepancies.

The next step is to ask the coachee to draft a brief cover letter, inviting people's feedback. You ought to provide them with the following guidelines:

- Indicate the exercise's scope.
- Request help for your development.
- Give general instructions (such as the scale used).
- Secure a deadline.
- Indicate that the responses are only seen by the coach.
- Provide the coach's email address.
- Ask them to mention their working relation to you.
- Thank the participant for their help.

As you can see from the guidelines, confidentiality is highlighted and secured and there is no mention of assessment. Upon collecting the numerical data, you can utilise them to create focus and direction in working with your client's areas of development and supporting their strengths even further, without even disclosing any numbers. This stage is important. You can't work on everything.

Emphasise strengths and weaknesses (or areas for future growth and development). Find one or two things to work on, rather than a whole bunch at once, even if your client seems to be interested in changing many things. Prioritise if necessary. One thing at a time.

(Peltier, 2001, p. 17)

From time to time, I opt to leave out part of the instructions (usually the part where they request that the participant indicates their working relation with the coachee). Some coachees will *proactively* ensure that this information reaches me. Overall, I will risk creating experimental situations to extract information about my client, and hope that by understanding my intention, this will not jeopardise their trust. It is up to each coach to decide for themself if this is a game they want to play. Nonetheless, extracting *process observations* is usually even more important than the survey results themselves. We will be exploring the all-important topic of process versus content within the next few pages.

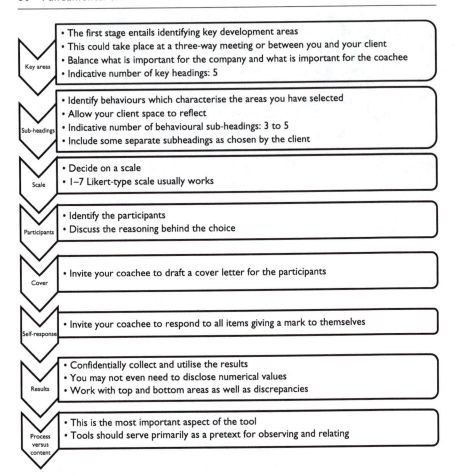

Figure 4.2 The customised 360-degree survey

Psychodynamic competencies and the use of self

During the early stages of my career as a coach, part of me wanted to hide my psychologist's hat. It is a fact that *there is (or there can be) a distinct difference between the quest for meaning and self-actualisation and the quest for maximising performance and increasing profit.* It is also a fact that several colleagues with a background in psychology have struggled with this notion as they moved into coaching. There is, however, an additional indisputable fact: When it comes to understanding people and their patterns (behavioural, psychological and other), there is no professional background that can match a mental health professional's advantage. The reason, other than mere experience and training background, is simple: Your whole demeanour revolves around converting the self into a function capable of receiving and analysing *data* from and about the client and providing these back to them as *feedback*.

Not everyone should have to study psychology to enter coaching; at least not for the whole 7–10-year cycle. However, it is vital that coaching training programs include a strong self-development, psychological component. This component can give coaches a strong edge in delivering their services. I have witnessed this with my trainees over the past decade. The depth of understanding and the application of such conceptions should match and reflect the coaching rather than the psychotherapy practice; and be closely monitored and supervised by a senior practitioner. However, if someone is serious about taking their coaching work to the next level, then they should have at least a basic understanding of psychological phenomena in the consulting room, which they should aim to develop over time. And I am not talking about NLP here, which is what coaches with a limited psychological background resort to first. I am talking about the more difficult, less linearly methodological, stuff.

During my time as a coach trainer, the four psychotherapeutic concepts that I have found to be of great use to me as well as my trainees, and which I wish to share with the reader, are:

- separating process from content;
- transference and countertransference;
- Projective Identification;
- parallel process.

Conveying and explaining these concepts to trainees over a year-long post-graduate training (which includes ample opportunity for practice, dialogue, reflection and supervision) has been a challenge. It is even more so on paper. However, someone has to take the risk and make a start.

The most important thing to remember, whilst trying to grasp the essence of these concepts, is that they are useful in providing us with hints and tips, *more often for our own internal use and direction and less so for disclosing to the client*. In addition, their usefulness is maximised if the data they yield can be cross-validated with information we have already collected.

I will proceed to present these psychological concepts in their basic form, adjusting their use and application to executive coaching on occasion, supporting the content with real examples either from my practice or the practice of my supervisees and trainees.

The *use of self* in generating data (as well as in the consultant's presence, which will be explored in the next section) is the fine line that separates an adequate coach from an excellent coach. We find out things about our client from three sources.

1   *The story:* This is what our coachees tell us about themselves and, needless to say, it is likely to be fairly biased.

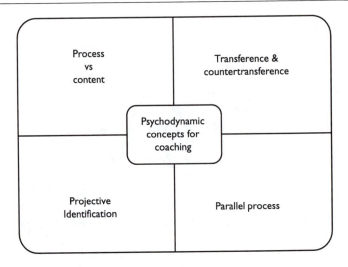

Figure 4.3 Psychodynamic concepts for executive coaching

2   *Other people's story:* This is how others perceive our coachee and even though this information could carry a little bit more weight, since it reveals more about the impact they have on others, it is still *second-hand information.* This includes past assessments, past and current 360 surveys, performance appraisals, etc.

3   *The coaching relation:* This includes our **observations, reactions and feelings** about the coachee as things unfold during the coaching process. Even though it is clearly open to bias, it is indisputably *the only first-hand piece of information* we will ever get.

Process versus content

Consider our tailor-made 360-degree survey as described above. Its primary purpose is to generate data with regard to how others view our coachee and their impact. *Or is it?* The fact is that you and the coachee have undertaken to complete a project, requiring a high level of synergy, the exchange of feedback, adhering to deadlines, inviting the support of others, managing time and resources . . . the list goes on and on and on. It is not very far from a complete business case simulation at worst and an absolutely realistic business scenario at best. Not such a bad set-up to find out how your coachee functions in real life, is it?

For example, what if everyone gives excellent marks to a coachee (including themself) with regard to their promptness and consistency, and at the end of the day, they have been unable to secure a single report on time? What if everyone indicates how great they are at managing time and resources and they have been late for most of your meetings? Let's not focus on negative discrepancies alone, though. What if everyone indicates a distinct lack of proactivity and initiative and your client has taken the time to record and share excellent process notes regarding your sessions and collected further feedback about themselves from three more colleagues?

There are no right and wrong answers to the above questions. It may be that the respondents really like the participant and are unwilling to share challenging feedback; or that they fear others might have access to it. If the feedback your coachee has received appears too harsh compared to how you have perceived them during the coaching engagement, it may mean that the system has not supported your coachee enough or has underutilised them (or that something needs to be calibrated within the system, which is something that an Organisational Development Consultant should be able to assess and provide feedback on). As already indicated, a coach *is* first and foremost an OD Consultant and we will expand on this concept in Chapter 6: Systems-focused executive coaching.) The perfect, right answer is of secondary importance. What is of primary importance is that you have generated data worth exploring; and it is these very discrepancies one should look out for. *The art of being able to* **separate content (what is being said) from process (what is taking place)** *can be the jewel in the competent coach's crown* and is the first competence that we can borrow from the world of psychotherapy.

Transference and countertransference

Contrary to popular belief, psychotherapy relies *as much on the here and now* therapeutic relation as it does on dwelling in the past. Very few people grasp why someone should have to understand why they are the way they are in order to get better. I partly tend to agree. There is little point in exhaustively tracing the archaic, early childhood roots of our behaviour (the typical Mummy- and Daddy-related stereotypical exploration) and modern psychology seems to understand this.

At the same time, very few people would dispute that we are primarily the product of our experiences and upbringing (together with genetics) and for executive coaching, we can just leave it at that. It is, however, worth considering that our past experiences have invited us to act and react in certain ways (some people would call this defences or limiting beliefs, others habits or survival mechanisms; and there are also those who comprehend that we do and become what we need to do and be, in order to be safe and evolve). Nonetheless, these little habits or ways of being have an impact on others; and as already mentioned, discovering more about this impact and perhaps partly managing it with deliberation can be an excellent coaching objective. *It should be deduced that the general impact that our client has on others (combined, of course, with the unique chemistry of our pairing) will also be the impact that they will have on us.*

I cannot, therefore, overstress the importance of understanding that this is the only first-hand piece of information that the coach will have available in relation to their client. In psychotherapy, this phenomenon is called *transference and countertransference* and it has evolved from being a problem for the therapist back in the day when Freud coined the term, to becoming a very useful piece of information for modern psychology practitioners more recently.

According to Clarkson (1993, p. 177), "They (transference and countertransference) occur whenever emotions, perceptions or reactions are based on past experiences rather than on the here-and-now."

You may notice the term "counter" before the term "transference". This is because it is a reaction to something, namely transference, whereby the client transfers (projects) feelings from their past onto the therapist (in this case, the coach), acting them out accordingly; and the coach responds. Transference is defined as the phenomenon whereby a past relation is repeated within a present relation and the emotions experienced are at least partly inappropriate to the present. For instance, a client with a history of controlling parents and feelings of anger around it may view her coach as an authority figure and therefore resist or sabotage (passively or actively) the relation. In their turn, the coach may react to the situation by exhibiting authoritarian behaviour outside their normal spectrum. In other words and as already indicated, since we are a product of our experiences and upbringing, these will also define our behaviours and habits.

I personally find it very useful to be able to understand where my patient is "coming from" (and I am obviously and distinctly referring to my psychotherapy practice here and not my coaching sessions) when I am the recipient of behaviour that reflects a relation they had in the past and has been described to me. It is also very useful to them, because when I – for instance – mention or indicate that they seem to protest to me about the therapy boundaries in a similar way that they protested to their father for not letting them stay out late, this triggers in their mind the realisation that they may be behaving like this (transference) on many other occasions to many other people; and this may be partly inappropriate and they may wish to review it and get over it. This kind of dialogue and exchange is, of course, *partly inappropriate for coaching* and there is no reason to collect your client's family history and extensive personal story. However, having some idea of their past circumstances, and how they came to be who they are, can serve as an invaluable internal compass. Overall, however, I avoid airing such thoughts in my time-limited coaching engagements. They are mostly for internal consumption and they should mostly remain so, especially for coaches with little or no training in counselling and psychotherapy.

In my opinion, transference does not just take place in a therapeutic relation; *it takes place throughout our lives every minute of the hour with every person we ever meet.* And by default, therefore, relations that extend beyond a certain duration will inevitably be partly based on transference and countertransference; and this includes the coaching relation. At this stage, several psychologists will protest extensively (if they have not already) about reading up on advanced therapeutic concepts in a coaching textbook and rightly indicate that these phenomena are unconscious, they develop and make their presence felt over a period of several years, and in the course of an intensive therapeutic relation, and there are more risks to consider than there are benefits. While there may be some truth in all this, after carefully observing the benefits of familiarising coaches with such concepts, I feel that this is a risk worth taking and its contribution in developing coaching can be immense.

As a coach, you will inevitably be exposed to behaviour which may be partly out of place and will, therefore, pose a discrepancy that you will be able to observe and experience. Even though you should try and minimise interventions connecting the present and the past, allowing yourself to openly experience and perceive your client's range of behaviour and emotions, and the impact those have on you, before supporting their calibration, will give you a head start in understanding them better; and such mental notes can prove invaluable in supporting your coachee's transformation.

Case study 3: "Daddy issues"

The executive, a young ambitious woman in her early 30s, is head of a major department in a shipping company. In the context of a long-term assignment with her company, I have been assigned to train and coach her. Despite good productivity and performance, and the fact that the executive gets on fairly well with her peers, when it comes to communicating with her supervisors, all hell breaks loose. Our relation is initially civil and fairly productive. As time goes by, my role in the organisation shifts and I find myself coordinating training sessions and board meetings for middle and upper management, which in some way gives me more authority (not executive authority, I must add; a coach/consultant should shy away from it) than an external consultant would normally have. It is not long before I am confronted with a ferocious and polemic rhetoric from my coachee, which I have only previously witnessed during meetings between the executive and her boss or while she is talking to me about him. During our coaching talks, I have come to know that her father is a high-ranking judge, a rather firm authority figure. Had this been a psychotherapy engagement, this would have given the opportunity for a rather fruitful intervention, since it is fairly evident that people with authority over the coachee provoke and reproduce feelings from the past. However, this would have been unacceptable in a coaching context. I therefore opt to follow a fairly safe route and during a heated discussion, marked by intense persecutory remarks from the executive towards me, I take her to the side and indicate that I am not her boss and that there is very little need for this kind of behaviour. For a moment, she seems to recollect herself and to be in touch with this realisation. Indeed, communication becomes less polarised for a while; however, the edge triggered by the shift in my role and authority never quite goes away. Soon after that I choose to end our coaching engagement, which I feel is appropriate both for the executive as well as for the protection of my own well-being.

This is one occasion where transference posed a serious problem, and one of the few where I chose not to work with it or through it. My internal compass in the form of my countertransference dictated that I remove myself from the equation rather than work things through. Needless to say, transference and counter-transference have worked in the coaching relation's favour on other occasions. If the relation reproduced has been loving, warm or collaborative, then the coach may ride this wave to their benefit. They do, of course, fall from a higher pedestal if things go wrong, so being cautious when things go too well too soon is highly recommended.

Observing the transference and countertransference, and being informed by them, is therefore the second competence that will help you generate data.

Projective Identification

The term identification in itself is useful enough and refers to the phenomenon whereby the client identifies with the consultant and vice versa. Such confluence can have a positive effect in terms of modelling constructive patterns and behaviours; however, it may also denote a fragile sense of self. The psychoanalytic explanation indicates that this is an archaic behaviour and originates from our infancy, when it is near impossible to have enough awareness about our own separate existence and therefore we perceive ourselves as a part of our mother or parents (or them as a part of us). Coaches are unlikely to work directly with or comment on a client's fragile sense of self; however, being able to understand the basic parameters of this phenomenon may inform and calibrate our interventions. For instance, a client identifying with us is unlikely to respond well to challenging feedback. Their fragile ego may require some massaging first; otherwise narcissistic injury and shame may compromise rapport forever. At the same time, specific issues that are symptomatic of a fragile ego, such as a difficulty in receiving feedback, self-critical comments, lack of confidence in decision making, etc., can be addressed within a coaching relation.

Melanie Klein took Freud's concept a step further and coined the term "projective identification" (Klein, 1946, p. 102), which refers to *an interactional activity designed to make the other experience the projection* (Bion, 1959). The aspects we project and assign onto others are, of course, primarily unwanted or repressed parts. One basic manifestation, for example, is when we see evil or negative in everyone and everything around us and we adopt the moral and sane side for ourselves. Projective Identification is a similar kind of *splitting*; however, it can occur *in an emotional and somatised way*. Paradoxically, it is worth adding that the phenomenon has also been described as the infant's defence against separating from the mother. As far as I am concerned, both interpretations make sense, but above all can be of use to coaches, especially the sensitive and empathic ones, since the phenomenon can account for emotions and sensations before, during and after sessions that may belong to the coachee, yet remain repressed and therefore projected.

Case study 4: Could you carry this for me, please?

My supervisee, a soft, empathic, gentle woman, reported feeling inadequate, stuck and angry after sessions with a particular executive. Whilst exploring the case, it turned out that the client appeared as particularly collected, cynical and almost detached both from the sessions as well as his professional role. Whilst exploring his history, I found out that the executive had been overlooked for promotion three consecutive times, had received a salary decrease and was reporting to a woman 15 years his junior. My supervisee had marvelled at his magnificent tranquillity and had classified it as a positive and resilient characteristic. Nonetheless, she continued feeling unable to progress further and experienced extreme tension before and after the sessions. When asked if she had explored the client's feelings with regard to his slow career progression, she indicated that she had not, since there was no indication that there were any. I pointed out that whereas it may not be our place as coaches to work with the client's repressed feelings, it is important to be aware that these will from time to time be projected onto us and we will be forced to carry them for our client. Recognising the Projective Identification may or may not be of direct benefit for the coachee; it can, however, liberate the coach by helping them recognise what belongs to whom, and this internal shift can in itself be of great importance in the coaching relation. Indeed, my supervisee tuned in and this enabled her to be more available to the client, since she was now able to better support herself. Within a few sessions, the client acknowledged his bitterness and instead of admiring the illusion of resilience, the coach worked towards co-creating an assertive development plan to speed up her client's progress.

Parallel process

If you have struggled with the previous three concepts, despite my efforts to simplify, contain and adjust them for the coaching practitioner, you need to brace yourself even further for this one. Observing and understanding the parallel process is a skill that the seasoned Organisational Development Consultant cannot go without. As repeatedly mentioned in this book, coaching outside the context of Organisational Development is like trying to build a basketball team with players who train separately.

Grasping the concept on a purely theoretical basis is fairly challenging; however, I am optimistic that this section will create the circumstances for the reader to reach a hands-on awareness. I can still recall the first occasion when I caught a glimpse of a parallel process. The impact of the realisation was extremely powerful.

For those of you who have watched the movie *The Matrix* (Lana and Lilly Wachowski, 1999), you may recall a scene where a crewmember observes page after page of binary code – the matrix – being downloaded onto several computer screens.

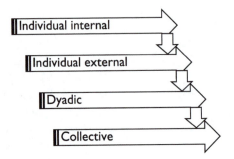

Figure 4.4 Parallel process

Our movie hero, Neo, approaches the crewmember and asks him if he always looks at the code. After all, what he is seeing is a bunch of meaningless 0s and 1s running from the top to the bottom of the computer screen. Whilst pointing his finger at various points on the screen, the crewmember turns to Neo and without hesitation, says: "I don't need to see the code. All I see is blond, brunette, redhead, blond, blond, brunette . . .". The ability to identify the parallel process is similar to being able to decipher binary code and *extract the exact information you need.*

The phenomenon of parallel process refers to the replaying of the same pattern within at least two of four settings: individual internal (our psychological processes), individual external (our life and actions), dyadic (dyadic relation dynamics) and collective (groups, teams, corporations, etc.). The phenomenon seems to be exacerbated when the relevant process (or business) is unfinished.

Case study 5: Certainly uncertain

During the early stages of my career as a coach, I worked with what I experienced as a very passively resistant client. Even though he would turn up at meetings on time, produce the work we had agreed on and maintained a polite and civil demeanour, I felt that I had to fight extremely hard for every inch of progress we ever made. Upon completing each cluster of our work, he would just sit opposite me, expressionless as if he was expecting me to signal our next task. There was no reaction, no reflection, no initiative and no positive or negative feeling. A couple of sessions before completing our cluster of six meetings and frightened by the prospect of having to continue for another six like that, I openly announced that I felt there was nothing I could do to help him and despite the lack of any obvious resistance, I felt I was carrying the weight all on my own and conducting the session all by myself. After a long pause, it occurred to me that our dyadic interaction could possibly be a repetition of something that was happening for my client on a collective level and took the initiative of asking him if he also felt stuck and helpless in any setting. He responded by confessing that having recently been selected for promotion amongst a team of executives he was now managing, every day he walked into his office uncertain of what he needed to do next, what the company required of him and unable to delegate any of his work to his team. Indeed, he continued, "I feel completely stuck but I have no idea what to do about it. After all I am the supervising officer and I should know what should come next better than anyone". The revelation came as a relief, I imagine, for both of us and we were then able to focus our coaching collaboration towards requesting and receiving support from his team and openly sharing his need to receive assistance. This was an example of the coachee's collective process being paralleled into our dyadic coaching relation. Often, the repetition of the parallel process is our client's unconscious yet most effective way of conveying to us what is happening for them, by doing it rather than by talking about it. As such, it can serve as a very useful little hint, especially with regard to unspoken or even subconscious material.

The Gestalt Cycle

Fritz Perls' revolutionary psychotherapeutic approach stands tall, especially amongst the humanistic disciplines. Its origins, which include classical psychoanalysis and philosophy, and its by-products, which include NLP, are far too numerous to mention. Anyone wishing to deepen their understanding of the approach in relation to business and organisations should read Ed Nevis's text, *Organizational Consulting* (1987), considered a bible in the field. For the time being, we will examine its primary data-generation tool, the Gestalt Cycle and explore its applicable parameters for executive coaching.

If there is one thing that Gestalt insists on, that is *totality*. Gestalt, being a German word, does not translate very well; however, the closest one can get to providing a definition is "wholeness" and "completion"; and this is precisely why it has proven so popular and so useful within the context of Organisational Development and consequently executive coaching. After all, this is precisely what we do as coaches: create the circumstances that enable our client to bridge potential gaps and therefore maximise the flow of their potential.

The Gestalt Cycle displays this experiential flow in a very sensible and matter-of-fact manner, which can apply to pretty much any activity, from drinking water to completing the most innovative of projects:

The example of drinking water is always a good place to start and you may want to try and work on it, once I have guided you through a typical business task. Let's work with the concept of attending to emails that require your immediate attention (*unfinished business* is a favourite Gestalt concept, since it epitomises incompletion and therefore a fundamental challenge to be tackled during coaching).

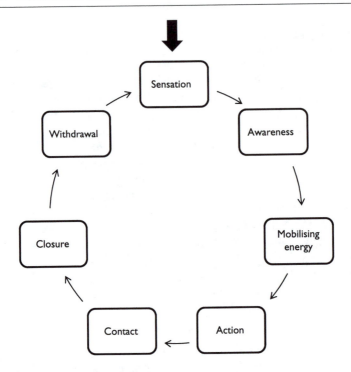

Figure 4.5 The Gestalt Cycle

Following the cycle above: A vague, worrying *sensation* seems to gently, yet persistently and consistently, emerge within your consciousness. The fact that several important emails are standing by, requiring your attention in your inbox, inevitably reaches your *awareness*. You *mobilise your energy* and turn to your laptop screen. You take the *action* of opening your inbox items and you make *contact* with your objective of replying to each pending message. Once you are done, you press "send" and your task comes to a *closure*. You *withdraw* from your desk and walk away with a *sense of satisfaction,* ready to face the next challenge.

You can probably deduce that you can apply the Gestalt Cycle to pretty much any activity; also that cycles happen within cycles, some never even take off and some never complete; and this is where it gets interesting for executive coaches. Observing, identifying and comprehending *interruptions* to the cycle can greatly support your client's effectiveness, quality and speed of delivery, thus rendering them a better executive and leader. Let's go through those interruptions and try to understand more about them.

Desensitisation is the interruption that takes place just after sensation and hinders awareness. It indicates a fair amount of repression and decreased sensitivity. The consultant may be able to observe this interruption if the client does not present "natural" reactions to certain events, such as expressing anger at

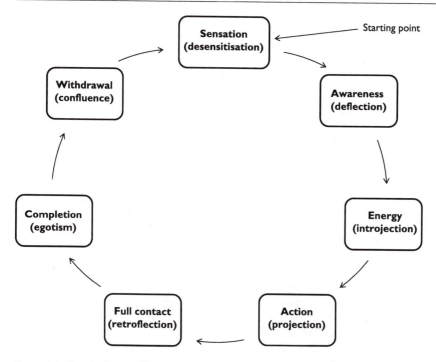

Figure 4.6 Gestalt Cycle interruptions

something they perceive to be very unfair or enthusiasm for great potential opportunities. It is my belief that Projective Identification, as presented earlier in the chapter, qualifies as desensitisation. The coach gets to experience what the coachee refuses to. A desensitised executive can be very difficult to communicate with (since you can't really figure them out) or be running the risk of a sudden and unpredicted emotional outburst, or worse yet, health problems. Such topics can provide excellent ground for coaching exploration.

From time to time, we will become fleetingly aware of our sensation; however, we will choose to divert our attention to something else before we mobilise our resources. Our friend from the example above, the one with the pending items in their inbox, could easily choose to divert their attention to something else (like organising their paperwork, or going out to lunch). I am sure we all recognise this kind of avoidance and procrastination, which also take place when we change the subject during an inconvenient conversation. *Deflection* can be very costly for executives and a seasoned coach should not deflect from addressing the issue.

An *introject* is the equivalent of NLP's limiting beliefs. It refers to our pre-established value system, sense of self-worth and overall view of the world and the ways in which these stop us from acting, taking risks and achieving excellence. Identifying and exploring your coachee's introjects takes skills and expertise as well as a fair amount of "Sherlock Holmesing" around their positions, until you reach the core. "I am not good enough", "Everyone around me is an idiot", "Nothing can change" are typical introjects. Absolute terms (never, everyone, nothing, etc.) are a good hint for snatching the end of the thread and unravelling it for your client. Introjects stop us from pursuing excellence and a coach should focus on that area for their client and challenge them with dedication, commitment and valour.

By now you should have a vague idea of how *projections* work. If it is not convenient for us, we pass it onto the "other". This splitting act separates us from the collective and deprives us of a lot of influence. We usually tend to occupy the good side of the fence and place everyone else on the dark, negative side. It is the coach's task to enable the client to recognise their own shortcomings as well and support them in understanding others and developing some empathy. Otherwise, our client will spend the rest of their professional life feeling self-righteous, yet isolated and unsupported. It is easy to identify a client who projects through the constant judging and criticising of others or even the reverse projection of idealising others and self-diminishing. The coach needs to focus on calibrating this contact-inhibiting tendency. We will explore the concept of working with polarities in Chapter 5: Transformational leadership.

The epitome of *retroflection* (literally meaning turned back into one's self) is depression. Classical Gestalt theory advocates that retroflection is anger and negativity turned inwards, due to the fact that we cannot express it or act it out towards others (either due to circumstances or introjects or even desensitisation) and therefore we do it to ourselves. Self-harm, or even suicide, is also another example of retroflecting; however, so is finding comfort in isolation (because others will not provide us with it). So what does that have to do with coaching? Those clients who retroflect will present with a "stormy stillness" about them. The coach's task upon identifying the retroflection is to actually provide some pacification and model that it is safe enough to "come out" through a solid, secure coaching attachment. For dealing with retroflection, it is actually more important *how* we do things rather than what we do.

For those of you interested in exploring matters further, it is worth mentioning that, in my opinion, *egotism* is linked to narcissism. Executives who are preoccupied with observing themselves from the outside, rather than actually participating or making contact, are difficult to relate to. Executives need a certain degree of egotism, of course, to rise up the corporate ladder; however, too much of it will alienate those around them and, worse yet, will deplete the executive of valuable resources that come from celebrating the completion of something. Burned-out executives often suffer from egotism, and the primary area of focus for the consultant is to support the executive's pace and ability to make contact primarily with themselves and then with others. Again, modelling such a relation within the coaching context can be immensely useful and the consultant may wish to make themself visible, available and "real". Sharing some of your process through feedback (such as indicating that you feel left out of the relation or something to that effect) may invite the executive to take a step back. Taking a step back and pausing is a good start. It's about pace, permission and relational capacity.

Confluence (literally meaning the junction where two rivers meet and in some ways the opposite of retroflection) refers to the difficulty of separating and going at it alone. We will explore the relevant concept of individuation – that is, belonging yet being separate – in Chapter 5: Transformational leadership. The primary indication that our client is struggling to experience themself as a separate autonomous entity is a difficulty in maintaining boundaries (time, financial and other) and a tendency to present themselves in union with other entities (the company, colleagues, you as the coach, etc.). Even though this "we" attitude is not an all-negative characteristic (i.e., it can enhance loyalty and alignment with company vision as well as "compliance" with the coach's wishes, perceived or actual), it is not exactly the best way forward when it comes to leadership characteristics such as accountability, decision making, risk taking, etc. It is not difficult to spot the confluent executive; however, if you feel that mere behavioural interventions and techniques (such as time management) will suffice to bring about improvement, think again. The phenomenon needs to be comprehensively approached and identified, and doing so without shaming your coachee or causing further defensive allegiance to the collective requires advanced, psychological skills, good rapport and patience, lots of patience. At the same time, an executive with an inclination to form confluent relations may try to form one with the coach. If the coach resists, this will ban them outside the sphere of trust. If they give in, then a silent conspiracy to avoid challenge and the production of meaningful work will be established. The latter is a very frequent phenomenon and is often disguised in the coach and coachee walking away, pretending they conducted some serious work, whereas in fact they simply safeguarded each other's narcissism.

Giving and receiving feedback

> If you want to be right, set up criticism vacuums; if you want it to work, implement feedback loops.

The definition of feedback as provided in Impact's Diploma in Executive Coaching and Organisational Development is the following: *"The art of conveying meaningful data and observations to your client in relation to their behaviour, with the aim of supporting their growth and improvement"*.

With regard to the coach's skills, it would be fair to presume that *giving feedback* constitutes their primary deliverable. The competencies we have presented so far (establishing rapport, listening and generating data) are absolute prerequisites to being able to inform our client about the impact of their behaviour, before helping them to improve it. At the same time, *receiving feedback* from our clients helps us find out where they stand with regard to the process and progress of the coaching relation. It is vital that these skills become second nature to us, almost in an automated, involuntary way.

We should not simply model these skills to our clients; we should be *teaching* them how to successfully accomplish them; for an executive can only lead their team by delivering feedback towards their growth and can only improve themselves by receiving feedback with regard to how they are perceived.

The good news about delivering feedback is that, like listening and unlike rapport, it can be directly and methodologically presented, and this is what we will be doing next, for the most part based on the Gestalt approach. The key concept that the seasoned coach needs to acquaint themselves with is the concept of *phenomenology*. A central theme for the Gestalt approach, *phenomenological observation* revolves around *collecting and presenting information, which is indisputably present within our consciousness*. In some ways, it could be argued that if this were an exclusive position, psychology, which is based on accessing and interpreting the subconscious and unconscious, would be rendered rather obsolete. A rather blunt statement; however, an equally true one, for that matter.

The methodology presented below manages to achieve something which is as impressive as it is effective: It combines utilising internal feelings with external events to generate useful data for the coachee. Throughout the past two decades, teaching and training people in the art of providing *phenomenological feedback* has never failed to generate a feeling of gratitude for the brilliant tool that has been given to them; and this is true even for the toughest of customers (which included myself back in the mid-1990s, when my mentor, Bernd Leygraf, first introduced me to Gestalt techniques).

Let's go through the 5-step methodology:

1   The first prerequisite in delivering effective feedback is to take advantage of the *here and now*; that is, to deliver feedback whilst something that you wish to observe is taking place between you and your coachee. This is the primary ingredient, which renders your position indisputable and self-proven.

2   The second step is to *present a couple of past occasions* when your client exhibited similar behaviour. This is a good time to *combine* data from various sources. For example, if your observation can be further supported by the outcome of the 360-degree survey or by the feedback – transparently – shared by your coachee's supervisor or HR Manager, then you will have created a very strong case. This particular approach works very well for groups as well, whereby each member takes on a familiar role and rides along with it. Chapter 6 (Systems-focused executive coaching) will expand on role allocation within systems.

3   The third "move" requires some disclosure from the side of the coach and it is best if you have established some rapport before sharing your own process. It entails letting your coachee know about the impact their behaviour is having on *you*. This is a fairly bold move, and if used appropriately, it can serve a multitude of purposes: It can model taking risks, it can greatly enhance rapport, it can promote transparency and, of course, it can permit and facilitate the exchange of feedback. In my experience, this is usually the trickiest, most

intense, challenging moment in the coaching relation, at least in the beginning of your career; it is, however, also the most fruitful one. Once you take this risk for the first time, there is usually no going back and if you have been remotely successful in sharing your internal process with your client, the quality of the relation increases exponentially, commitment and engagement become mutual and a synergistic alliance is established.

4   The *link between the here and now relation and the external* (which is, after all, what you are working on) is the inevitable next step. After all, the coaching relation is used as a *simulation*; the quicker you grasp this concept, the faster your development as a coach will be. It would be unlikely that the impact that the coachee has on you is only felt and experienced by you. It is most likely that colleagues, friends and clients have the same reaction. You should therefore present your coachee with this *assumption*. If your coachee is aware of it, then this is a good time to discuss the pros and cons of maintaining this behaviour. If they are not aware of it, then you need to give them space to reflect. It is also time to find out if others have shared similar feedback with them. Assuming that you have not been completely off the mark, then it is slightly worrying that no one has ever taken the time and care to share feedback. This may have something to do with how your client keeps others at a distance or may well be an organisational issue (again, a coach with lack of knowledge regarding Organisational Development and systems would have limited capacity to address such phenomena).

5   Generating data and enhancing awareness create a solid platform. If this were psychotherapy, it would for the most part suffice. In coaching, however, direction and action need to be launched; and if the client does not ask, "So, what do we do now?", it is the coach's responsibility to initiate this conversation and *trigger the co-creation of an intervention*. This is the time to be creative with your client and to come up with ways that will gently create a shift (rather than force a change) in your coachee's less productive patterns. Assign some homework proposing alternative behaviours; encourage the collection of further feedback; devise an experiment; if working with a team, support the creation of peer-coaching couples, responsible for monitoring each other's progress. The possibilities are endless.

Case study 6: I know this. That. And the other. I

Rationalising, explaining or justifying your behaviour will usually not change its impact . . .

My client, a successful executive in her early 40s met with me in the context of a project designed to support middle management towards empowering the company's future leadership potential (present performance as well as future succession planning). She began the session by indicating that she did not fear feedback and was willing to hear anything that I wanted to tell her. After all, she was always willing to receive feedback, "she did not care what others thought of her". Upon completing the initial 360 (which, as I have indicated, is primarily a pretext for creating relational circumstances), I took some time to go over the results and worked through the responses on items that required some attention. Each time, I was the recipient of a rather long monologue, which consisted of extensive rationalisation, lengthy disclaimers and sophisticated positioning. The monologues, primarily intended to defend my client's position, served a purpose in throwing me off and it was not long before I lost interest as well as focus, coupled with a mild sense of irritation. The worst part was that my irritation was not sufficient to keep me engaged. As usual, I decided not to react on my feeling and decided to let some time go by in order for me to reflect on things.

Limited budgets meant that the number of sessions was down to four, a rather small number for producing results. I therefore had to act fairly quickly. Session one had been about co-creating the 360, session two had been about going over it. Since session four would be a follow-up, my only choice was to attempt my intervention in session three; or do nothing at all: After all, technically we had worked on a few 360 items (such as the ability to secure support and the ability to utilise adversity which had received fairly low marks by comparison) and one could argue that I could consider my coaching assignment fairly successful and complete. This would, however, render me an average coach and the truth is that I would rather take a risk of failing altogether than accept that. I therefore proceeded to interrupt one of her usual monologues and disclose that:

"Every time I ask or question something, I receive a series of long disclaimers. As a matter of fact and despite how intelligent the response may be, by the end of the monologue, I am so disengaged that I am hardly aware what the conversation was all about. This is what is taking place right now and it has also taken place several times already during the first two sessions (I named a couple of occasions). I feel like I am trying to dribble down a basketball court with a basketball covered in grease; by the time I am ready to take a shot, I am so tired, all I want to do is hit the showers and go home. I wonder if you have received this feedback before and if other people around you feel the same way. I also wonder if this is partly the reason that the item 'The executive is able to receive support' got a low mark on the 360. I find it very difficult to 'pin you down' and as such, I find it very difficult to provide you with any support. If all this is somehow true, we may want to consider the pros and cons of this pattern and perhaps devise an intervention that would bring about a conducive shift for you, your relations, your influence and your career".

Despite it being a fairly long monologue from my side, the intervention, eventually, hit the spot. The executive recognised her difficulty in securing support (though it would be long before we touched upon her fear-based need to be right and not feel "caught out or exposed") and we devised, initially, a feedback collection scheme, whereby trusted colleagues were invited to let her know every time she engaged in her familiar monologues. Since this is still work in progress, I do not yet have a definitive outcome; however, what is important for you is to grasp the technique of providing phenomenological feedback combined with transference feedback (how the executive makes you feel).

Before concluding the section on giving feedback, it may be useful to share some tips in bullet-point form:

- Don't take it for granted that your coachee wants to receive feedback. Ask first.
- Present your opinions and assumptions in context and not as facts.
- Give feedback on one issue at a time. Usually, there is one central theme anyway.
- Set your tone to suit your client's style and personality.
- Timing is of the essence: too soon and rapport is lost. Too late and sensitivity is hindered.
- Focus primarily on the behaviour and then on the person.

And, of course, remember that unwanted feedback can be shaming and traumatic. Everyone has their own pace and style and, according to John Whitmore (1992, p. 150): "If resistance persists, coachees are either resisting being more aware or being more responsible." Which conveniently moves us on to the next section.

Receiving feedback should form part of the coach's (self-)assessment and should take place unofficially throughout the coaching or consulting engagement and officially, perhaps even statistically, at the end or during the follow-up phase. Did the coachee find the sessions useful? Did you challenge and support in equal measure? Was the outcome sustainable? Was rapport established? We should be open and try to receive feedback in a non-defensive way. After all, if we wish to pursue excellence, we need to constantly improve. For the narcissists among us, this is a good framework that will render our shortcomings bearable.

At the same time, it is vital that we "train" our clients in the art of collecting feedback. It is rare that I do not assign this task to my coachees after the third or fourth session, even after a 360 has been conducted. Written statistical surveys cannot replace a face-to-face exchange, and an executive proactively seeking to improve is far more powerful than an executive who has been assigned to collect feedback through a tool in the context of their coaching assignment.

The first thing I convey to my clients, especially the ones with a tendency to engage in endless defensive rhetoric regarding feedback they have received and the circumstances surrounding it, is that *regardless of how well we explain or rationalise our behaviour, its impact remains the same.* There is a very specific beginning to a sentence, which allows us to diagnose that someone is about to *fight feedback* (or helpful suggestions and recommendations): It goes something like this: *"Yes, but . . ."*

It is my opinion that this "Yes, but . . ." is possibly the most counterproductive position ever adopted (and yes, I have used absolutes deliberately in this statement). Eric Berne (1964) expanded on the theme of "Yes, but . . ." in his landmark text, *Games People Play*, concluding that a series of "yes, buts" leads either to silence or forces the recipient of the "yes, but" to agree with the – usually stubbornly helpless – position of the "yes, but-er".

The trick here is to engage in the "yes, but . . ." dialogue for just about long enough to produce a respectable volume of "yes, buts . . ." (verbal or other), so as to be able to provide phenomenological feedback (as presented in the section "Receiving feedback") to your coachee. The seasoned consultant will be able to separate process from content and instead of labouring away on constructing their feedback or position, will turn the focus of the interaction on the *resistance* rather than the actual content. The example below aims at illuminating the issue of fighting feedback.

The coachee, a talented IT executive in his late 20s, complains to the coach that his manager is "always on his case". The 360, as well as the interaction between the coach and the coachee, has indicated a heavy tendency to miss deadlines, lack of respect for keeping boundaries and lack of willingness to align with business procedures.

Coach: *I wonder if your time-keeping challenge is what's making your manager persecute you?*

Coachee: *Yes, but there are so many other priorities.*

Coach: *Do you proactively discuss what those other priorities are?*

Coachee: *Yes, but we have a different opinion on the matter.*

Coach: *Perhaps you should make a case for your position and incite her to reflect on your suggestions. Do you want to think about how to do this here with me?*

Coachee: *Yes, but she never listens and anyway we don't have time for such meetings.*

Coach: *It sounds like there may be an organisational issue around setting priorities or promoting alternative approaches. Would you be able to voice and explore this at a management meeting?*

Coachee: *Management meetings are not about new ideas; they are about on-going, urgent projects.*

You have probably deduced that this dialogue could go on for a very long time, and the unfortunate coach could end up spending a whole session trying to support the coachee in working out a solution through a combination of delivering feedback and providing suggestions. Believe me when I say that thousands upon thousands of hours of coaching have been wasted in this fashion, and several coaches have left sessions with the sense that they have conducted their duty, yet feeling strangely bruised and battered. Don't become one of those coaches. Draw your client's attention to their resistance and tendency to fight feedback and go as far as asking them if they want to work with you and *whether it is more important to be right or successful*. It may sound somewhat confrontational and it probably is; however, you will never get far with a coachee who does not know how to receive feedback and is not even aware of it.

There are three basic parameters you need to convey in order to enhance their ability:

1   Indicate that receiving feedback creates the circumstances for observing ourselves.
2   Underline that being able to observe ourselves and the impact we have on others *bridges the gap between our intention and the outcome of our actions*.
3   Present the advantages of being able to deliver deliberate leadership interventions by being in a position to assess how others will react to you.

This is also often the premise with which I engage my coachees during the kick-off meeting (whether it is the first paid one or a "chemistry" meeting). If the coachee is unwilling to work by receiving feedback, there is little point in trying to deliver a coaching intervention. The vast majority of coachees and potential coachees get it and this initial exchange usually creates excellent, clear and transparent circumstances for the future of the collaboration.

Chapter 5

Transformational leadership

The coach's disposition

Throughout the presentation of *Skills, Method* and *Presence* in this text, I have repeatedly emphasised the importance of *Disposition*, of "being" over "doing" and how this affects the coaching relation. The coach cannot support the coachee's evolution to a place much further than where they themselves have arrived. It is my position, that this place is conquered within rather than claimed externally. Before presenting this chapter's content, I must share a story; a story that provides some context; and context, in coaching and leadership, is of vital importance.

Professor Renos Papadopoulos

Whilst wavering over the future ledge, remember to navigate with yourself as the compass.

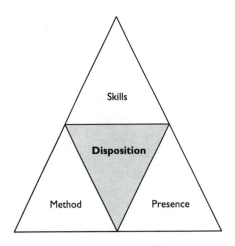

Figure 5.1 Disposition

Several years ago, as a fresh alumnus of my post-graduate psychotherapy training, living and working in London, I sought and found a clinical supervisor who matched my needs at the time. Fascinated by Carl Jung's theory (for very different reasons back then than now), I conducted research on identifying the right person to oversee my clinical work as well as support my understanding of Jungian theory. My journey led me to Professor Renos Papadopoulos. In addition to sharing an ethnic origin with me (which always helps, especially when you live in a foreign country), Renos was a Professor of Jungian studies at a university, a consultant for the United Nations, a Systemic therapist, a member of staff at the Tavistock Clinic, an author . . . the list just seemed to go on and on.

Youth's naïveté and oblivion around danger and risk as well as the fledgling man's narcissism played a very important role and after a few weeks of trying to secure an appointment with him, in 2002, I finally found myself sitting in his East London consulting room, where, no doubt, several senior practitioners, consultants and therapists (of twice my age, probably, since at the time I was 27 years old, and most certainly featuring significantly more experience) had sat before me. I calmly presented my training background, clinical load and business context, all of which he seemed to ignore completely as very useless information and a few minutes before the end, he asked, in a rather bemused way, "Why do you want to take up supervision with me?" to which I readily – much too readily – replied, "I want to be the best there is". He laughed, probably as I have never seen him laugh over the past 15 years I have known him, and sent me on my way, telling me we should *both* think about it. I was thrilled just to have come so close to securing a supervision space with such a senior mentor and was already dreaming of the wealth of Jungian theory that this man would decipher for me. He eventually accepted me. For the next 4 years (until I left London, that is), Renos helped me develop, not in a way that I did not think possible, but in a way that I did not know existed. Throughout the duration of our engagement, *he did not employ or utilise a single Jungian term once*, despite my efforts to lead him there. He was kind enough to assign a wealth of Jungian literature for me to read and allow me into some of his public lectures. When I left, in 2006, I could understand little more about the Shadow, the Archetype, the Persona, the Collective Unconscious, Synchronicity and several other Jungian concepts than I had picked up from my newly acquired, and rather challenging, Jungian book collection. I could, however, write a detailed book on the statement that had driven me to Renos 4 years earlier – "I want to be the best there is" – and on the notion of *not understanding*.

In 2012, I was determined to share my "understanding" (or lack of it) of Jungian concepts and integrate them into coaching practice; locally at first and globally in due course. This is still the plan and this is why this chapter is here. Renos was by now an external associate for my consulting firm, still supervising me from time to time, delivering selective workshops and scrutinising my work. I must have caught him in a good mood, because he agreed to support the creation of a coaching workshop that would integrate and utilise Jungian concepts. Either that, or my intention induced considerable anxiety that I might make a right mess of it, which would see 50 or so executive coaches, participants of the workshop, talking endless nonsense about Jungian theory after attending; publicly. When I threatened to include the module in our Diploma in Executive Coaching and Organisational Development, I could hear the sirens of fire engines all the way from London to Athens. Trepidation is a great motivation and it earned me a few good web conference sessions with him.

Just days before delivering the workshop to an audience of more than 50 executive coaches, consultants, executives, Diploma alumni and more, he wished me "good luck", though he clarified that he "is not responsible for what may happen". The workshop was delivered; successfully. I received lots of encouraging feedback about taking such a risk and many people followed up wanting to find out more. A good 10–20% of the participants were so enchanted that they wanted Jungian theory to play a central role in their life. It wasn't all great news though. Throughout the seminar, I also received fierce attacks (sometimes unrelated to the topic), was challenged on several fronts and there were several attempts to steer away from Jungian studies into other, conflict-ridden, polarised areas such as issues of supervision, accreditation and other controversial material.

It was November. I returned home and lay on my couch, not getting up until the next morning. As a matter of fact, I did not "get up" for a good 6 months. Once again I had gone in oblivious to how powerful this material can be and I had paid a price. Jungian material threatens homeostasis and as humans we tend to become very resistant, unconsciously resistant to *transformation*. As I write these lines, I recognise this and I also understand how threatening and unsettling, unconsciously unsettling, the material must have been for a segment of the audience. Fortunately, the presence of alumni, colleagues and friends created a good-enough protective shield, and I managed to see the workshop through to the end, before dragging myself home. Some people close to me indicated I had risked great exposure. I felt I had taken an unprecedented beating. This is probably what my mentor had in mind, when he said that he did not want any responsibility.

In 2013, I delivered the module to Impact's 6th Diploma intake in Greece. Everyone, including me, escaped unharmed and very much inspired, almost enlightened I may add. I have delivered the module at least another dozen times ever since. It is always demanding, challenging, frightening, makes a major impact, and every time, I travel just a little step further, alongside the participants. This has led me to take the risk of including this material in this text (as well as in every Diploma intake ever since). Coaching must benefit from Jung's approach and the Myers–Briggs Type Indicator (MBTI) simply does not do sufficient justice to it. The good news is that Jung's position deals primarily with internal disposition; therefore, *you don't really have to learn how to do something*; you don't even need to learn how to think in a certain way. It is all about being; and this is what should distinguish the average coach from those seeking excellence and taking the necessary risks to reach it.

And Renos taught me lots about "being". He taught me that the – Individuation – journey never ends; he taught that often you will take a battering and that you need to metabolise that into Adversity Activated Development and resilience; he taught me that important things, such as conflict, are complex. He taught me pace. He taught me that smart terminology and method should not, cannot, replace essence. And more; a lot more.

It is my duty, therefore, to take yet another risk – as I did when I stepped into his office and as I did when I presented this material for the first time – a more conscious and conscientious one this time; and try to convey to you as much of what he taught me, throughout this book and in this chapter in particular, as I can manage.

Chapter synopsis

I have not placed a synopsis, especially not at the beginning, in previous chapters. However, Jungian material can be complicated, complex, multidimensional, confusing and unsettling. I have not once delivered the relevant training without strong reaction, direct or indirect, usually positive, yet at times also challenging. I therefore always kick off by indicating that I just wish to convey five things and *five things alone*. This helps and provides some context and safety in what would otherwise be an even trickier topic, even in the simplified form that I have devised for use in executive coaching. Each principle has a corresponding heading below:

1   Our *Epistemology* (our fundamental belief system) determines our *Position*, which determines our *Actions*: Therefore intervening on action alone is insufficient.
2   Occupying *polarities* breeds *conflict*. Both internal (intrapsychic) and external.
3   The *Archetype* has two polar sides. We normally focus on just one, be it for ourselves or for others. This results in an amputated, incomplete stereotype. *Individuation* is our life-long journey towards integration of Archetypes.
4   *Symptoms* are neither good nor bad; they are *synchronistic* opportunities. Therefore we can create meaningful interrelations by acknowledging additional dimensions.
5   The first casualty of splitting and oversimplification is *complexity*. And it's a vital casualty.

Epistemology–Position–Action

Is it our task to intervene on a deeper level and generate awareness with regard to our client's model of the world, or would supporting behavioural transformation suffice?

I hold an absolute and a relative position in relation to the above question: Coaching is about generating action; therefore (and contrary to psychotherapy, where generating awareness and internal meaning may suffice), our intervention ought to be practically manifested. At the same time, dealing with behaviour and behaviour alone means that the core factors, which have created it in the first place, remain unexplored and untouched. It is therefore my position that unless you touch upon your client's belief system, values and theorem with regard to how the world goes around, you will only succeed in fixing symptoms. The disclaimer here, of course, being that the exploration of such elements ought to remain (again contrary to psychotherapy) on a fairly superficial level. The definition of "superficial" in this case depends on a variety of factors such as your professional background and expertise (mental health practitioners will inevitably dig somewhat deeper here, whereas coaches with a business background hold an advantage in optimising professional output); the client's willingness, disposition and request; the time frame and several more, which you will need to assess for yourself. The core set of values and beliefs (according to psychoanalysis, as formulated and dictated by our environment by the age of 7) can be described as our *Epistemology*. In its turn, our Epistemology determines where we *Position* ourselves within various systems and circumstances. And finally, our Position, to a large extent, defines our *Action*. This neat model, presented to me by Professor Papadopoulos, can be your guiding light with regard to the aspects that you and your coachee wish to address. The focus for coaching should be on behaviour, which is primarily a conscious aspect of our existence; and for psychotherapy on Epistemology, which is mostly a subconscious and at times unconscious aspect. Position, in my opinion, is important in both cases, since it determines how we fit in with the collective; and this is, in any case, a vital component of life. I present it diagrammatically as Figure 5.2.

At the same time, it is the consultant's duty to reflect upon their own Epistemology and to scrutinise their own tendency to polarise and claim the monopoly of self-righteousness. As a matter of fact, this is the place to start and the place that gives you some prerogative to challenge your client. After all, this text advocates that it is near impossible to lead anyone further than where we have been able to go ourselves.

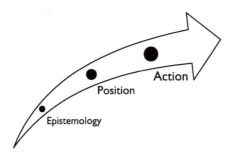

Figure 5.2 Working on a deeper level

Case study 7: I know this. That. And the other. II

A few years ago I decided to embark on a rebranding/restructuring/reinvention process in relation to Impact with the help of a friendly external consultant. Being a boutique consulting firm as well as a pioneer in providing Coaching Training and Organisational Development services both in the UK and Greece, it was not very difficult to adopt an elitist, segregationist identity. Even though some healthy narcissism can serve an organisation – as well as an individual – and its purpose, snobbism will not; and though I could not put my finger on it, I knew we were paying the commercial price for it, by distancing potential clients.

The consultant requested that we present the traits that separate us from the competition in as bold and polarised a way as possible and then supported us in presenting "the other side". The results were enlightening, to say the least, and greatly supported the organisation's transformation from introversion, self-righteousness and almost bitterness to interaction, empathy and respectful dialogue. I strongly recommend that coaches go through this process first, before trying to apply it to their client.

Identifying polarities and managing conflict

When two positions are fundamentally and diametrically antithetical, then each one is implied in the other.

Clear, black and white distinctions provide a sense of safety in the same way that belonging does. This is partly the reason why we are so eager to use and apply tests and assessment methods and trick our way into classifying people. The MBTI is a fine example and it is no coincidence that apprentice coaches request assessment and diagnostic tools more than anything else at the beginning of their career. The relief (and authority) that comes from labelling will never lose its charm and it is worth considering how this very characteristic of human nature has actually written the world's history. It is important that coaches understand this, and it is even more important that they understand how *polarities* follow a parallel process (please see Chapter 4) and are therefore as much a part of ourselves as they are of the cosmos.

More often than not, we will choose to occupy the sane, moral, justified, smart end of the spectrum and leave the shady aspect vacant for everyone else. Humankind's natural tendency is to observe themselves as "better" than they actually are and view their position more favourably. During this process, we may choose to pick some people for "our team" (usually those that are in agreement, complacent or non-threatening) and place others diametrically opposite us. The limitations that this disposition presents for coaches and coachees alike are as numerous as they are dangerous. The scope that becomes available, once freed from it, is immense.

According to Carl von Clausewitz in his epic strategy manual, *On War* (2007, p. 193): "Where two ideas form a true logical antithesis, each complimentary to the other, then fundamentally, each is implied in the other."

Or, as the Chinese would put it, *the reverse side has a reverse side.*

One of my favourite opening questions when coaching executives is to ask them whether they feel they are getting what they deserve. Many will respond by indicating that for some reason or another they deserved more, and for some reason or another they did not get it. This reason is usually related to others or how others "unjustly" perceive or undervalue them. This is an immediate polarity. It is "us" versus "everyone else who got what was ours" and "the high-powered, evil monsters that kept it from us", because "we" are "too smart", "don't sell ourselves well" or "don't comply well with the system's – unfair – rules"; because "we are more special than everyone else". The question does not only reveal the polarity with regard to the work environment. In the vast majority of cases, it indicates the client's overall attitude with regard to adopting opposite positions, as well as their inclination for *conflict,* both internal and external. This is an invaluable piece of intelligence for the consultant and a useful aid in trying to understand their client and their Epistemology.

Polarities can often expand into triangles. A fairly well-known concept in systemic psychology, which has found its way into coaching, is Karpman's *Drama Triangle* (Karpman, 1968). The Drama Triangle presupposes that the *victim–perpetrator* polarity will very often attract a third entity: the *rescuer.* This concept is of particular importance to the coach and they would do well to render its understanding part of their disposition.

The rescuer position is more often than not assumed by the newest, extra-systemic (external) arrival. That's usually the coach. The rescuer position holds a seductive and righteous power, and it is not too difficult for the coach to be swayed by their client's misery and form a confluent (please see Chapter 4: Fundamental skills: "Generating data"; "Psychodynamic competencies and the use of the self"; "The Gestalt Cycle") alliance with their coachee. It is all very friendly and cosy; however, there are two risks at play here: The first risk is that with the coachee absolved from any responsibility and accountability regarding their victim status, any chance of progression and integration, as described above, is seriously hindered. The second risk is that these roles tend to rotate according to the system's needs, and it is possible that the coach moves from the rescuer's position into the perpetrator role (and following that, perhaps the victim's); either through their own volition, due to their subconscious frustration with their client, or through the client's eyes, since their rescuer is not really rescuing them from . . . themselves.

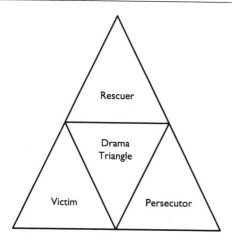

Figure 5.3 The Drama Triangle
Source: Derived from Karpman (1968).

The Archetype and Individuation

Individuate; instead of being what you do, try doing who you are.

- How do I separate myself from others?
- What do I resent and judge about others? Could this also be part of myself?
- How do I keep myself safe and separate by adopting the moral/sane/right position?
- What is the cost that I pay by maintaining this position?
- What would happen if I shifted my position?

The list can go on and is only limited by your creativity.

The basis of the above exploration can be traced back to Jung's theory around the *Archetype* (which in turn was very much influenced by Plato's *forms*). The Archetype is the primordial image that exists within the collective and individual consciousness and maintains psychological order. In other words, it is a subconscious classification system, which groups and shapes patterns and behaviours, often through personifying them. Some common Archetypes would be *the hero, the old wise man, the harlot, the money-thirsty boss* and many, many more. As indicated above, it is safe and convenient to create conscious and unconscious classification systems and to position ourselves on the "good" side.

By gaining a better understanding of Archetypes and opening up the possibility of observing their darker side, which Jung called the *Shadow*, we can benefit from a more holistic understanding of things and people as well as ourselves.

According to Jung, in his iconic text, *Man and His Symbols* (1990 [1964]):

> *If the shadow figure contains valuable, vital forces, they ought to be assimilated into actual experience and not repressed. It is up to the ego to give up its pride and piggishness and to live out something that seems to be dark, but actually may not be. This can require a sacrifice just as heroic as the conquest of passion, but in an opposite sense.*
>
> (Jung, 1990 [1964], p. 175)

The purpose of such exploration is not to shame and humble our clients or ourselves into admitting our imperfections. The purpose is to integrate our parts into a whole and equip our clients and ourselves with the awareness that will support a deliberate increase in performance and productivity; which partly, yet clearly, distinguishes the coaching objective from the psychotherapeutic objective of fulfilment and meaning. The process of integration of polarities was called *Individuation* by Jung. Effectively the process never ends and it determines the extent to which we can be happy with ourselves, whilst being a healthy, functioning part of the collective.

As Carl Jung succinctly puts it (1966):

> *Individuation has two principal aspects: in the first place, it is an internal and subjective process of integration and in the second it is an equally indispensable process of objective relationing. Neither can exist without the other, although sometimes the one and sometimes the other predominates.*
>
> (Jung, 1966, p. 234)

Exploring the Shadow side of our clients in a creative, curious and liberated manner can be extremely fruitful. One aspect that I like to draw their attention to is the archetypal dichotomy between the *Persona* and *the Authentic Self*.

There has been a lot of talk recently in business regarding Authentic Leadership and this text has made ample reference to its dimensions and usefulness for the coach. However, little or no attention has been drawn to the Persona, which is the "outfit" we put on in order to connect, relate, avoid rejection and generally adapt and survive. Jung describes it as "the individual's system of adaptation to, or the manner he assumes in dealing with the world" (1968, p. 122).

My feeling is that this derelict, and perhaps shame-stained, aspect of an executive's personality is very much neglected. Whereas companies unashamedly focus on branding, advertising, market research, etc., it would appear that individuals ought to shy away from deliberately (or less so) fabricating an agent of the self that will get things done better and faster, whilst making the lives of others easier. The secret, as with all archetypal polarities, lies in attempting to bridge the two; and for that purpose I have devised and used a matter-of-fact questionnaire, which I have found liberates my clients from the new age guilt of *not being themselves all the time* (Chapter 9: Coaching for impact: "Tell me about your Persona" hosts a briefer version of it):

1   How do you want others to perceive you at work?
2   How congruent is this with how you really feel?
3   How congruent is this with what you want to do and achieve?
4   How congruent is it with who you really want to be?
5   What are the benefits?
6   What is the cost?

The difficulty and challenge of being ourselves, yet belonging, is summarised by Carl Jung in the autobiographical *Memories, Dreams, Reflections* (1995 [1963], p. 377): "But anyone who attempts to do both, to adjust to his group and at the same time pursue his individual goals, becomes neurotic."

A second aspect that is currently worth exploring is the potentially antagonistic and polarised split in the *Anima* and *Animus* archetype. According to Carl Jung:

> For a woman, the typical danger emanating from the unconscious comes *from above,* from the "spiritual" sphere personified by the animus, whereas for a man it comes from the chthonic realm of the "world and woman," i.e., the anima projected on to the world.
>
> (Jung, 1968, p. 317)

He also says: "Although the two figures are always tempting the ego to identify itself with them, a real understanding, even on the personal level, is possible, only if the identification is refused" (1966, p. 261).

The two positions above tell us more or less everything we need to know to utilise this concept for our coaching practice. Let's begin by clarifying that the Anima and the Animus do not refer to gender, but to characteristics, predisposition and archetypal motifs. In other words, temperaments that we have historically identified as Animus-oriented would include strong, brave, orderly, etc.; and correspondingly for the Anima, those would include intuitive, empathic, creative, etc.

At this point in time, individuals and corporations are facing a number of challenges, due to the inability to integrate the two. Some of my observations would include female leaders being pressurised to only exhibit Animus characteristics (thus suppressing their Anima advantage of being creative, intuitive, flexible, etc.); male leaders struggling not to appear too domineering (thus suppressing their Animus characteristics, such as being decisive, daring, brave, etc.); corporations resorting to being controlling, absolute and directive in order to deal with uncertainty (thus suppressing their Anima characteristics of being inclusive, open, innovative, etc.) as well as many more.

Our job as coaches is to help our client identify their Anima and Animus characteristics and support them in creating a balance, which is neither reactive nor complacent. This would serve both their Persona as well as their Authentic Self and would further support their Individuation.

Figure 5.4 Ouroboros: The snake eating its own tail

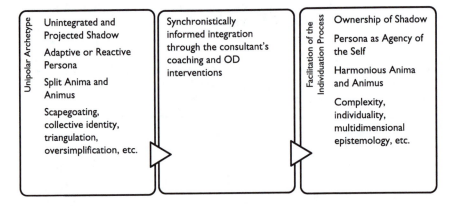

Unipolar Archetype	Facilitation of the Individuation Process	
Unintegrated and Projected Shadow Adaptive or Reactive Persona Split Anima and Animus Scapegoating, collective identity, triangulation, oversimplification, etc.	Synchronistically informed integration through the consultant's coaching and OD interventions	Ownership of Shadow Persona as Agency of the Self Harmonious Anima and Animus Complexity, individuality, multidimensional epistemology, etc.

Figure 5.5 The Individuation Process

Utilising symptoms synchronistically

Identifying and solving problems holds a special place in human collective consciousness. It is in part what gives specialists their mystique and power. Doctors, mechanics, plumbers, psychiatrists, even; without discounting their value and contribution, it is fair to say that the significance of their role is very much dependent on the need for diagnosing, alleviating and removing *symptoms*. It is natural that the amateur executive coach will sense the power and charm behind this trait and be drawn to it.

"What's wrong with me, doctor?" is a question I receive in various forms day after day. It takes some experience and internal stability to shy away from putting your expert hat on whilst proceeding to explain the "ins and outs" of the case as well as how you intend to "take care of things". After all, you are well "equipped" with several personality and aptitude tests, performance appraisal tools and other diagnostic aids; as well as precise, structured approaches and methods that hold the "answers" to the "patient's" prayers.

It is a fair play. After all, seven out of ten requests for a proposal shipping out of HR departments to coach's inboxes will request exactly that: a structured, tried-and-tested method that will alleviate symptoms and turn mice into lions. And as a coach, you should be able to present something structured, methodological and easy to understand in order to maintain communication on a level they can comprehend, generate the opportunity for them to benefit from your services, and for you to expand your client base. However, this is a chapter on how the seasoned coach nurtures and utilises a disposition that enables them to take matters further than a mere troubleshooter would; as far as being able to generate opportunity and strong direction from what at times may appear as a weakness or a threat (which, by the way, is exactly how SWOT ought to be employed as well).

According to Renos Papadopoulos (2006, p. 31): "We can understand phenomena not only in terms of them being effects to previous causes (this would be the Aristotelian 'efficient causality') but also in terms of their purpose and 'final cause' – their goal."

If you can grasp the above concept and, in turn, put it into action, you will be enabled to evolve from a mere troubleshooter to an *Agent of Transformation*; more importantly, you will have drastically intervened in your clients' "wiring" (the wiring that connects their Epistemology with their Position) and you will have made a difference; not simply on tackling current challenges but on equipping them with life-long resources.

Our clients (private and organisational) will often present us with the difficulties they wish to overcome; the obstacles that stand between them and their objectives. Such obstacles are the difficulty in managing time, the challenge of securing resources, the complexity of securing support, the inability to delegate, the power-lessness of articulating vision, the misalignment between performance and mission and many, many more. In typical fashion, we frequently respond by pulling out a project management-esque methodology that aims at removing the hindrance; one at a time. It is my position that even though this is an acceptable response, especially when applied by novice coaches, advanced practitioners should aim at achieving more. A lot more.

Symptoms are manifestations of an internal, often subconscious, reality, conflict or status quo. It is the same when the body's temperature rises in response to a bacterial infection. Even though the antipyretic medication will provide the patient with comfort, it will not in any way influence or eliminate the cause of the issue. As a matter of fact, one could argue that if science did indeed have the capacity to eliminate fever altogether, it would probably be a bad idea to do so; in the same way that it would be a bad idea to numb the sensation of pain.

Symptoms occur for a reason and eliminating them without understanding them is not just risky; it is plain counterproductive.

So, how should we go about supporting our client's utilisation of individual and collective symptoms? In the early 1920s, Carl Jung became interested in a phenomenon he labelled *Synchronicity*. The theories he developed were influenced by his acquaintance with the likes of Professor Albert Einstein, the Chinese *I Ching* (*Book of Changes*), physicist and Nobel Prize winner Wolfgang Pauli and many, many more people and ideas, probably including some related to parapsychology. Understandably, the depth and breadth of these studies are probably unsuitable, perhaps even antithetical for business coaches and consultants, including, of course, myself. I have, however, in the past been able to support hundreds of my clients and trainees by employing, and admittedly adjusting to fit, the simple, perhaps simplistic, core of Jung's proposed position. I am very keen to provide a trigger through this text, through this particular chapter and through this particular sentence, for you to understand, embrace, utilise and proactively yet naturally operate within a synchronistic context in your executive coaching practice and perhaps your life. I had better start with the definition of Synchronicity, then, as proposed by Jung himself in his homonymous text, which he only published in 1960, practically 30 years after embarking on this expedition:

As its etymology shows, this term (synchronicity) has something to do with time or, to be more accurate, with a kind of simultaneity. Instead of simultaneity we could also use the concept of a *meaningful coincidence* of two or more events, where something other than the probability of chance is involved.

(Jung, 1973 [1960], p. 104)

In addition:

It (the idea of synchronicity) is based on the assumption of an inner unconscious knowledge that links a physical event with a psychic condition, so that a certain event that appears "accidental" or "coincidental" can in fact be psychically meaningful.

(Jung, 1990 [1964], p. 291)

I don't know about you, but I can't think of a better coaching intervention than the one that utilises two or more events (fortunate or unfortunate) from the coachee's working life, supports them in extracting meaning and creates future, harmonious *direction and action*.

Needless to say, Jung did not elaborate on Synchronicity with the business world in mind and did not apply the concept to comprehend or utilise symptoms, but to generate meaning from this strange type of coincidence. I also believe that in his mind, Synchronicity included a fatalistic element, with a focus in the past, leading to revelations for those who were sharp enough to put the pieces together. For instance, having a conversation about someone that you have not seen for several years and bumping into them the next day, would be a typical synchronistic event; and you would be invited to decipher the significance and receive the hidden message from this event and perhaps take an appropriate course of action or understand something that has been revealed to you.

It is fairly clear that we will need to deviate somewhat heavily from the original position in order to fit the theory to coaching. However, the benefits we can extract are simply too good to miss and I am confident he would approve of this heresy.

In coaching, even though we heavily rely on collecting past data in order to understand patterns, our focus lies ahead and our gaze points to the future. Our aim is to proactively generate future action and direction, by relying, in part of course, on data from the past. We cannot avoid obstacles and hurdles; we can, however, put them to our service in the same way that sailboats have mastered the wind regardless of its direction.

It may be best to illustrate with an actual case study.

Case study 8: Constructive sabotage

Z. is a successful C-level executive, working for a multinational retail company as a Regional Director. He has evolved fast and his numerical performance and appraisals over the past few years have put him firmly in the fast lane. However, this has recently somehow been brought to a halt. His company has offered executive coaching sessions to the whole of the Senior Management Team and Z. and I have ended up together. He is a challenging individual, with a predisposition for conflict and a feisty character. However, once I passed the initial test with some straight talk and by providing him with plenty of applicable support in managing his "internal pace" and temper, our working alliance (lasting to this day) was firmly established and we embarked, well on our way for co-creating success and strengthening performance. Our work took place mostly at the company's headquarters, which were in the same city as my office, when he visited from his base, which was hundreds of miles away.

As with most coachees, I decided to co-design a personalised 360 survey and distribute it to some of his close associates, so as to identify possible discrepancies between how he thought other people perceived him and the actual impact he had on them. Even though we continued to identify and work with several presenting issues and opportunities during our sessions, we allocated a fair amount of time to designing the 360 survey, which he kept on his laptop in order to work on it in between sessions. So when the time came to finalise and distribute it (in the 9th or 10th session out of a total of 12), I was in for a surprise when I arrived in his town for a site visit to find out he had lost his laptop, and of course all its content, and he did not appear too concerned about it. Therefore, the actual product and object of our meeting was now missing and was impossible to reproduce within the remaining time. On top of all that, it was one of the few times that I had to go to his town (3 to 4 hours' drive away). Naturally, I experienced some disappointment; however, the immaculately appalling timing screamed that I would either make some synchronistic sense out of this to support myself and generate direction for my client, or waste our meeting and perhaps a large chunk of what we had gained up until that point.

I therefore devised and resorted to an internalised synchronistic questionnaire:

Table 5.1 Questionnaire

What purpose does this serve?	For my coachee	For the coach	For third parties (e.g. for the company)
Past Knowledge (utilise event to identify or confirm patterns of the past)			
Present Action (utilise the event to mobilise resources and action)			
Future Direction (utilise event to generate future direction/intervention)			

Our exploration yielded some of the following explorations, assumptions and outcome:

Table 5.2 Questionnaire outcome

What purpose does this serve?	For my coachee	For the coach	For third parties (e.g., for the company)
Past Knowledge (utilise event to identify or confirm patterns of the past)	Do I subconsciously sabotage myself and my progress at crucial points in time, to the point that I consider this a natural occurrence?	How ready and willing am I to creatively and flexibly deviate from my original plan of action and how do I manage my disappointment?	Could the company be collaborating in creating circumstances that create a sense of overload and resentment that will from time to time create upheaval?

What purpose does this serve?	For my coachee	For the coach	For third parties (e.g., for the company)
Present Action (utilise the event to mobilise resources and action)	How can I secure support and help, create circumstances for synergy and display versatility?	What alternative course of action am I being invited to follow and could this be a superior course of action that I have been missing?	Do we need to consider alternatives for this executive?
Future Direction (utilise event to generate future direction/ intervention)	What process, patterns or habits is this incident inviting me to review?	Will this process add something to my future repertoire of interventions or render me more prepared?	Do we need to rotate or promote him to extract maximum value, or even let him go?

The absolute answers to the questions are of secondary importance. What is important is the shift that this approach encourages, both for the coach as well as the coachee. Instead of focusing on the historical why and how something happened, (which is what coaches "accuse" psychoanalysts of) or trying to come up with solution-focused behavioural interventions (which will resolve one problem, one time), the synchronistic approach focuses on the purpose our behaviour serves, thus liberating us from the guilt of "correcting our wrongs", reframing stagnant negatives into active positives and working with who we are rather than with what we do. The gentle power of *Transformation* is bound to produce a more sustainable, progressive shift than the brutality of diagnosis and change; and can be a particularly effective instrument in the hands of the executive coach.

Acknowledging complexity

One could argue that this is the executive coach's primary asset; and perhaps the one that we try to trick our way out of most often. Personality profilers, aptitude tests, assessments, standardised techniques, step-by-step guidelines and methodologies and various other "recipes" are devised and employed with a single purpose: to dismiss the uncertainty of *complexity* and the unpleasantness, the Shadow if you will, that this may cast on our coaching work. It is a tempting proposition and it puts things neatly into their little boxes. As a coach, however, you need to ask yourself: Is this good enough? Not just for your client (who may in their turn also seek the safety of the recipe), but also for you.

It is not very difficult to know when you have avoided complexity in your work. All you need to do is sense the historical, confluent, conspiracy involving you and your client and the sense of relief when the work is over and the curtain falls behind the reciprocated congratulations. On the other hand, if you have taken the risk of acknowledging complexity, you may have not arrived at neat conclusions and solutions; you will, however, have worked relationally, addressing who your coachee is (rather than what they do), and the end of the work will be marked with the sense that your journey may have well continued; even though you both did the best you could *for now*. A closure involving happiness and sadness, satisfaction and disappointment, achievement and incompletion indicates that both you and your coachee have taken yet another little step on a never-ending journey.

Whilst running the risk of oversimplifying matters, it may be worth proposing a general direction for introducing and utilising complexity during our coaching work.

Beware of:

- splitting symptoms, characteristics, people (including your coachee) and phenomena into polar good and bad, moral and immoral, sane and insane, etc.;
- not acknowledging, exploring or at least suspecting people's dual, archetypal nature;
- relying exclusively on technique and methodology;
- not considering the pros and cons even during the most unequalled triumph or the most unprecedented disaster;
- overly identifying with or overly opposing your coachee's position (please see Chapter 4: Fundamental skills: "Generating data": "Psychodynamic competencies and the use of self").

It has been argued by many that we should keep clear of such "psychoanalytic" concepts in coaching. I beg to differ. I appreciate and have personally experienced the experts' caution around misusing or abusing advanced concepts. I also share the amateur and the non-psychologically minded coach's fear of entering deep, unchartered waters. At the same time, I hold a firm belief that coaching ought to evolve and draw benefits from longer-standing, more established disciplines. The trick lies in being able to manage this transition respectfully and with the right pace and direction. The current generation of coaches has an opportunity to pave the path for the next one.

This chapter on transformational leadership has been an attempt to touch upon the concept of *Individuation for Leaders*, both for the coach as well as the coachee. For they are both leaders. Despite it being yet another multidimensional, complex and almost mystical Jungian term, securing a basic understanding of its parameters may serve as a beacon light for those of us involved in supporting other people's development, whilst striving for our own.

Chapter 6

Systems-focused executive coaching

It is this text's non-negotiable premise that we cannot interact with individuals to affect their performance, unless we can master a fair understanding of the collective that surrounds them. Inevitably, we interrelate with what is around us, shaping and influencing it in the same way that it shapes and influences us.

For executive coaches, this principle is of paramount importance. *Companies recruit us to work with their executives, primarily in order to increase organisational output* and secondarily to support individual development. Regardless of how we choose to reframe or go around this (for example, by simplistically arguing that an increase in individual performance will result in an increase of group performance; or that individual executive values are aligned with collective, company values), there is no escaping the fact that *unless the executive's development is relevant and aligned to organisational strategy, culture and direction, the impact of our intervention will range from "good enough" to plain counterproductive.*

Over the years, I have faced a lot of resistance from professional coaches regarding this notion; and I have fought back to support it in several ways; for example, by labelling Impact's training program the Diploma in Executive Coaching and *Organisational Development*. There are several reasons as to why an executive coach would prefer to shy away from their client's organisational challenges and opportunities. First and foremost, unless we are recruited to design an organisational intervention (including data collection, interviews, training, coaching, board coordination, systemic and structural interventions, leadership consulting, etc.), *we are neither getting paid nor being invited to expand beyond our one-on-one work.* I have learned this lesson only too well and have lost a fair number of bids and contracts that requested individual coaching services, by producing a more holistic proposal. I have also managed to alienate a CEO or two by providing verbal and written reports touching upon organisational issues, rather than sticking to individual issues regarding my coachees. I am certainly advising caution towards taking such risks. At the same time . . .

Should this be enough to discourage us from adopting a systems-focused approach in our work, at least when it comes to our internal values, intelligence gathering, interventions and predisposition? Of course not; for, despite the aforementioned risk factors, the main reason that executive coaches refuse, or fail, to see beyond their one-on-one work, is because they resist transforming their range of expertise and prefer sticking to what is known and familiar to them; and for executive coaching, the discipline that aims at breaking glass ceilings, this is simply not a good enough reason. Even if you are not inclined to work as an Organisational Development Consultant (and one could argue that the opportunity cost of doing so may, at times, prove too high), you should be able to comprehend the interactive, reciprocal, interrelational dynamics that exist between your coachee, their organisation and, of course, yourself. It is therefore the moral duty of this text, despite not being an Organisational Development guide, to provide the executive coach with a basic systemic framework.

An overview

The first thing to consider is what the term *System* refers to. The position taken by biologist Ludwig von Bertalanffy in the 1940s as a reaction to scientific *reductionism*, in my opinion, still stands today and is the one I use whenever I deliver coaching training, since it encapsulates key concepts:

> The meaning of the somewhat mystical expression, "the whole is more than the sum of parts" is simply that constitutive characteristics are not explainable from the characteristics of isolated parts. The characteristics of the complex, therefore, compared to those of the elements, appear as "new" or "emergent." If, however, we know the total of parts contained in a system and the relations between them, the behavior of the system may be derived from the behavior of the parts.
>
> (Von Bertalanffy, 1968, p. 55)

The key words in relation to executive coaching, as far as I am concerned, are *relations* and *interactions*; which is effectively what we, as coaches, are invited to optimise for our coachee, so that they can increase their influence and improve their system's collective performance. The key concept to understand is that every time there is a shift in one component within a system (for example, through our coaching intervention with one of its leaders), the arrangement changes and we have a new, emergent organisation.

One of my favourite examples makes reference to sports (which together with psychology and business constitutes the third major influence for coaching). Imagine a football or basketball team, whereby athletes are individually coached, with little regard for team tactics, no focus on their particular role or position, an individual mission and vision and no feedback from other team members. Now imagine being the coach. You may be able to produce the fittest, strongest, most enduring athletes on earth, but you will never be in a position to contend for the World Championship. This is what it's like to coach from a reductionist, individual coaching perspective.

Now imagine being the same coach, having access to the whole team; able to witness each athlete's areas of strength and areas of development in relation to others; empowered to intervene and coordinate when it comes to tactics and free to share or even co-create vision as well as feedback loops. By comparison, you will be a force to be reckoned with, won't you? That is the difference between a *systems-focused coach* and a coach who simply focuses on individual performance.

The above context gives rise to an even more serious consideration, which is the term *executive* coaching itself. I think it will not be long before the word "executive" is irrevocably challenged (both in the context of coaching as well as in the context of management), simply because it is *all wrong*. The term has come to refer to a member of the management team possessing the authority to execute decisions and implement strategy. This is clearly misleading, since it fails to encapsulate the fact that in order to "get the job done" and in accordance with the modern world's script (please see Introduction: "On influence"), no one can do this alone any more. Therefore they need to *lead*; and in order to lead (even in the case of leading by example), you need to rely on a system of which you are a part, with which you can communicate, relate and interact. It is therefore the coach's duty to be able to catch a glimpse of this and in their head, heart and soul replace the notion of executive coaching with the notion of *leadership coaching. We are primarily supporting leadership qualities as opposed to executive skills*; therefore this, naturally, places our coaching intervention in the realm of *Systems-focused Organisational Development Consulting*. However, the world is not yet ready for this, for several reasons, whose account will not add much to the reader's growth at this stage and as such will be omitted.

Prerequisites and circumstances

Before setting off to design and deliver your systems-focused coaching intervention, it is vital to secure the right circumstances for it. It is worth being aware that if the organisation is unwilling or unable to accommodate a systemic coaching intervention, you will have to make do with what you can achieve through pure individual work; or withdraw your services. It is, however, always worth presenting your client with the option of a systemic intervention. In my experience, some of the time they will appreciate it and support you; some of the time they will appreciate it, but will not be in a position to create the circumstances for it (which in itself lends itself to an organisational diagnosis); and on rare occasions, they will consciously or unconsciously view it as threatening and will want to see you out as soon as possible. In my opinion, this is a rare occurrence and worth the opportunity cost risk. However, it is best that you decide this for yourself.

Entry

As indicated in Chapter 2: Coaching methodology: "Entry", it is best to kick off the meeting in the presence of the CEO, the HR Director, the line manager and the executive. This provides the opportunity to align everyone's requests and observations, collect feedback and maximise your systemic impact.

Data collection

Involve people around your coachee (see Chapter 4: Fundamental skills: "Tools: The customised 360-degree survey") and find out how they view him/her, what they need from him/her and what their areas of strength and development are. If you have your coachee's consent, you may even choose to talk to a couple of them or even spend a day shadowing your coachee. Observing live interaction will yield useful information, not just about your coachee but also about the company.

Work with and for a team

If you are going to be coaching a number of people, request that you can treat them as a team, conduct a training session or workshop with them and create *peer-coaching couples*. Putting yourself in a position to do that is not just the optimum accelerator, but also the best way to generate sustainable results by generating rapport all around. Team meetings generate ideal systemic circumstances during which you can observe which role people choose to adopt, how they interact with different characters and how they collaborate, communicate, lead and overall co-exist. In other words, you are being given the opportunity to collect data and intervene *during an actual simulation of a working day*. Sharpen up your skills as a facilitator/trainer, design exercises that will reveal your coachees' characteristics, make real-time interventions, create circumstances for exchanging feedback and when you are ready to go, leave peer-coaching couples behind, rendering them responsible for each other's progress. For a seasoned coach, this will quadruple the effectiveness of the intervention, integrating your coaching work into an Organisational Development intervention and truly making an impact. The latest fashion is to call the utilisation of coaching skills for groups, rather than individuals, *Team Coaching*. I personally fail to see how Team Coaching can extend far beyond training a group of people in certain behaviours; for, *if data collection is involved, the intervention is customised; and if aligning collective performance with the company's vision and strategy is the objective, then the appropriate term to use is* **Organisational Development**.

Culture

Now I have conducted some preaching (to the converted, it is hoped) as to why you should strive to be a systems-focused coach, explored and challenged the systems-related semantics around executive coaching and touched upon how to create optimum circumstances for a systemic coaching intervention, it is time to actually look at some practical, methodological components.

One could argue that culture can make or break a company, since it refers to the values and behaviours company members employ in order to achieve their goals, or as Schneider (1997, p. 255) puts it, "The way we do things around here in order to succeed".

"[Research by] . . . Kotter and Heskett discovered that corporate cultures that are strong and effective have a *significant impact* on a firm's long-term economic performance" (Schneider, 1997, p. 254). This consequently marks its importance for the coaching intervention and directly places responsibility on the coach to understand and address it. Since culture is a collective phenomenon, it naturally falls under the realm of systemic thinking. In theory, the place to start is by securing the vision, the mission and the principles that the company abides by and observing the extent to which individuals (Senior Management, in particular) are aligned with them. In the event that a company has not been through the process of formulating the above, it may be a good idea for you to help them do so; provided, of course, that you have the background and training of an OD Consultant (in addition to your coaching expertise) and that they are willing to sponsor and support such work. In the event that you are working with the owner or CEO of a company, the vision, the mission and the principles of the company will inevitably form part of your coaching work. In other words, it is hard to escape working with and understanding the system that your coachee serves.

In addition, it is worth finding out more about a company's culture, especially if it is not an infamous FTSE 100 company, through the Internet – what they say about themselves, for example, on their website, but also what others say about them. However, as indicated in the section "Psychodynamic competencies and the use of self" (Chapter 4: Fundamental skills), this is the client's story combined with the story of the "others", and even though it is not a bad place to start, it is most certainly incomplete.

At the end of the day, the best way to comprehend a company's culture is by becoming involved with it. The way they approach you, the booking of the initial meeting, the front desk, the walk from the front desk to the office, the frequency, consistency and promptness of their communication, their time management, bureaucratic processes, speed of delivery and more, much more. Everything should be observed and recorded, and you should look out for repeated patterns and prominent themes, but most importantly, *discrepancies between who they say they are and what they actually do*. You do not need to feed back this information (unless you are hired to deliver an OD project, in which case this process will represent the backbone of your intervention); however, understanding it deeply will enable you to cut through the nonsense in your coaching work.

Once you acquire a fair idea of the organisational culture, your job is to equip your coachee(s) with the necessary tools to align themselves with it or, perhaps most importantly, lead its *evolution*. Even though companies try to maintain a versatile, inclusive culture, it is almost impossible for some of their characteristics to not be more prominent, and very often you will find that distinct traits may, to some extent, exclude their polar opposite: For example, a highly innovative company may pay less attention to discipline and institutions; NGOs may place a focus on commitment at the expense of structure; construction companies may prefer direct, candid communication at the expense of more subtle approaches. Even though we should avoid stereotyping, we should also be acutely aware of not appreciating diversity. A leader's job should be to strengthen their company's core culture and values, whilst at the same time challenging them. The coach's job is to support leaders in achieving that.

Case study 9: Groundhog Day

> Reciprocal relations are not based on unilateral gratitude; as such, they are not threatened by ingratitude.

The company is a medium-size family-run retail business that has evolved successfully in the past decade from a small team of 10 employees to a business of more than 200 employees. I have been assigned to coach the head of each department (six or seven executives) in order to provide them with the necessary leadership skills that will enhance team performance, whilst allowing the CEO to step back from micromanaging each and every product line. In essence, the hierarchical structure is flat with non-existent reporting lines; the executives are product rather than people leaders. The CEO's management style (effectively, the single reporting point within the company) ranges from the highly judgemental to an absolutely laissez faire attitude. The vast majority of employees complain and feel they have it worse than everybody else, especially when it comes to work load, reward and recognition; however, by 5pm, 90% of the company are out of the door, and it is clear that no one really understands or has any notion of what a demanding work schedule looks like, especially compared to executives of multinationals during the same period. In addition, no one ever resigns or is fired and those leaving the company very often return after a few years. The system is symbiotically balanced, resembling the perfect conspiracy.

My engagement begins with the majority of people moving their appointments with me due to other "urgent and important matters" and my arriving to find out I do not have a room to use. Any 3-way meetings between me, the coachees and the CEO end up in my resolving existing urgent and important issues and conflicts (admittedly successfully, thus setting things in motion); however, there is little mention of or opportunity to address the actual relationship, culture and long-standing challenges and malfunctions. This situation drags on for quite some time and even though my services remain in demand, my initial objective (which was a vague "increase effectiveness and collaboration") gets more and more out of sight. A few months later, I have practically turned into an HR Manager, dealing with recruitment, employee issues, an organisational chart and even compensation and benefit issues. Before I know it, a very long time goes by and for one reason or another, I am unable to withdraw my services (and it was certainly not because of the remuneration or other benefits). I am receiving very little to no appreciation and I begin to feel resentful. At the same time, I am focusing more and more on fire fighting and administration rather than supporting corporate strategy and overall performance. All my efforts to return to a coaching role and provide added value are sabotaged. It took me several years to actually (and yes, these are the words that I used at the time) resign, taking the opportunity when an executive I had nurtured and supported within the company, acted with what I perceived as ingratitude, a rather useful wake-up call. The cost had overall been high, yet the lessons invaluable.

The assignment sucked me into the system, in the context of a parallel process. Long-term engagements will often lead to such phenomena and these may from time to time be valuable, especially since the coach identifies with the company and gains a very deep understanding of how it operates. More often than not, though, you cease being an external consultant and you become part of the system; and this can take away your authority, your clarity and your ability to influence as an outsider. A consultant always works at the margins. Not in, neither out of, the system.

Meetings: The Optimum Systems Lab

We are not management consultants. Our understanding of the company's product, their marketing approach, their sales tactics and their overall operations does not need to be extensive. However, it cannot be basic and we do need to be able to understand it well enough for several reasons: being able to communicate with them; generating rapport; collecting data (content) that will enable us to observe patterns (process). As an executive coach, you will often be invited to work with individual members of the Senior Management Team and from time to time with the whole team. If you can gain entry into *Management Meetings*, this can generate a golden opportunity to optimise and multiply the benefits that your services can yield, given that you can maintain and support a systemic predisposition in your mind.

Below, I will share with you some hands-on interventions that have enabled me to support Boards and Management Teams, eventually saving them time, alleviating frustration, supporting collective rapport, promoting transparency and overall helping them move to the next stage.

The systemic premise dictates that components within an organisation interact in both linear and predictable ways, as well as non-linear unpredictable ways. In other words, there are things we control, things we may be able to influence and things outside our control; and this is a starting point that I very frequently resort to through a particular exercise, whether I am involved in individual coaching or working with a team.

Table 6.1 The exercise

Things I/We Control	Things I/We Possibly Influence	Things Outside My/Our Control	Unknown

Even though this appears like a simple, almost simplistic, exercise, it yields several invaluable benefits:

1   First and foremost, it brings about clarity, focus and direction by dispelling misunderstandings and promoting common ground for everyone. This also supports the building of meaningful *relations* by sharing commonly understood and accepted goals and challenges.
2   It saves organisations and individuals a lot of *time* and *resources*, primarily by removing the communication overhead of going over *data* that is potentially of no use.
3   Finally, it saves organisations and individuals a fortune on coaching *fees*. By separating the aspects we can do something about from the aspects we can do nothing about, our sessions, consultations and workshops will adopt a focused content and context.

If you are coaching a team leader, you may want to invite them to use this tool with their team. If you are coaching a team (Organisational Development), you may want to apply it during a meeting. I have personally discovered and verified that teams which successfully apply this exercise during meetings save up to 30% of time or breed the capacity to differentiate symptoms from causes. The exercise is an easy, practical, applicable way to begin; it will give you a quick win and increase your influence.

Following from that, you may be interested to find out more about which *role* everyone assumes within the group. For instance, in the context of the Karpman Drama Triangle, are they most frequently the victim, the rescuer or the persecutor; do they agree with everything that is being said or is every second word that comes out of their mouth "Yes, but . . ."; do they protest or do they propose solutions? It is important to be able to collect such data; yet it is even more important that you provide the relevant feedback to your coachee or coachees, for the most part in private, to avoid shaming them and generating unwanted trauma and resistance.

Establishing a *check-in* culture that invites everyone to share "where they are at" at that given moment is also another great aid. Trying to run a meeting when one member is recovering from bereavement, has just lost a very important sale or is feeling unwell for one reason or another, can be extremely challenging; especially if no one knows about it. At the end of the day, a check-in combines care and compassion with diligent data collection that determines how things are handled. Integrating goals and expectations for the day into the check-in can also serve in aligning them. Especially if the assumption is that these are common and commonly understood.

Promote a *Feedback Culture*. Revisit Chapter 4: Fundamental skills: "Giving and receiving feedback". Teach your coachees how to do it and help them build on it, with baby steps. Not only do you promote transparency and enable the unspoken to be revealed; you also empower executives to discover the impact they have on others and to align it with their intention.

Some additional guidelines that have supported my coaching teams and their members have been the following:

- Differentiate between Brainstorming and Operation meetings, with a focus on the latter, obviously. The overhead that is created when the two occur together is detrimental.
- Allocate a different chair for each meeting. This distributes accountability evenly, but most importantly, "teaches" people what not to do unto others.
- Eliminate the use of "Yes, but . . ." unless you have an alternative, applicable suggestion. At worst, replace with "At the same time . . .", which creates fertile ground for two opinions to co-exist in a non-antagonistic way.
- At the end of each meeting, allocate "who, what, where, when, how, with what resources, within what deadline, within which strategic context and with what tactical purpose". You will be surprised at the findings.
- Focus and report on results rather than on activities.
- Change the ratio of Questioning–Positioning–Proposing to lean towards Proposing–Positioning–Questioning.

Chapter 7

Coaching team managers

Today's business world is clearly in need of more effective management; and I am deliberately making use of the word management rather than its "sexier" synonym (leadership), because taking a highly-skilled, technically excellent executive, with little or no line experience from the IT, sales, marketing, research or other department, assigning them two, three or four reports, and expecting that they will lead before managing, is more often than not a recipe for disaster. In addition, today's business world demands that the transition from working solo to managing small teams takes place in the blink of an eye.

Arguably, our function, as executive coaches, is not to replace the learning provided by an MBA or MSc in human resources management (HRM), Project Management training courses or other academic or professional business training programs. Our job is to support leaders in becoming even better. In theory this is sound; however, theory differs greatly from actual practice and as you progress in your career, you will often discover that instances like the one mentioned above may, and probably will, form a significant part of your caseload. In addition, some distance separates academia and hands-on application. I therefore see no reason as to why coaches should not work with new or evolving team managers on basic management skills. Often, the more talented amongst these people will return to evolve as leaders. However, as Stephen Covey (1989, p. 145) put it, "First things First".

I believe there are four fundamental functions to attend to when coaching individuals who need support in managing their team: delegation, motivation, engagement and finally transformation, which is the stepping-stone in transforming from manager to leader. For the most part, these terms echo HR loud and clear, and one might be concerned about the possibility of stepping on the HR Director's toes, moving outside the coaching context, generating conflict and supporting management rather than leadership characteristics. I can assure you of two things: First of all, in my experience, the vast majority of HR Directors or other line managers, for that matter, will welcome your contribution, if it is well intended, adds value and ensures that they are part of the equation. Second, and congruent with the premise of this text, the complete executive coach is also an Organisational Development Consultant, who understands the system as a whole (please see

Figure 7.1 Coaching team managers

Chapter 6: Systems-focused executive coaching) and is therefore able to support the alignment of individual performance with the collective strategy. If supporting individual performance means focusing on management prior to focusing on leadership (and I can assure you that this will often be the case), then your focus should not be on doing what you think or feel you should, but on doing what you must.

Delegating

A weekly timetable consisting primarily of urgent and important stuff? Forget getting very far . . .

This is one of my personal favourites. Don't get me wrong. I like to control things around me as much as the next guy; if not more. I have painfully discovered, however, that I cannot be great at everything I do; and even if I was, there are not enough hours in a day to get it all done. Multitasking and the lack of focus it entails is not the way forward either. A coach ought to know that. *Delegation* entails *getting your strategic priorities right, securing support, developing talent, being excellent at what you specialise in and being authentic to yourself and others.* Explore this with your coachee and guide them to understand it. Still they may be unwilling to take the risk of letting go. Invite them to go through this list with you, which might make things a little easier for them:

- Establish a *delegation pace* that you are comfortable with and minimises risk.
- Secure *interactive communication* and a level of reporting that works for all parties.
- Clarify the shift in *responsibility*.

- Do not delegate *indiscriminately*.
- Strike the right *balance* between delegating tasks and authority/control.
- Delegate as a sign of *trust* to high performers and ensure that success is appropriately rewarded and recognised.

Motivating

A natural continuation of engagement, *motivation*, as far as I am concerned, is based on *giving people reason to excel*. In an age of lost values, salary and personnel cut-downs and tight deadlines, it seems almost impossible to find time to do that. This is where a coach comes in very handy. Presuming that you have entered coaching because you love giving people *reason to excel*, your task now consists of not just motivating your coachee, but also equipping them to motivate others. After all, this is what leaders do and to a greater or lesser extent, it is expected that leaders have sufficient capacity to self-motivate, especially when the going gets tough. With reference to Self Motivation, Daniel Goleman (1995, p. 47) states that it is directly related to "delaying gratification and stifling impulsiveness". In my view, this is also related to our ability to maintain *pace* and we will explore this concept extensively in Chapter 8: Leading with PRAID.

One of the most challenging scenarios that you may find yourself in is doing all the right things to give your coachee reason to excel, week in, week out, only to discover that they have, once again, turned up for their next meeting deflated and discouraged. I had to battle this scenario a few times in my career so far and I can vouch that it feels like a rather compromised position to be in.

Case study 10: Get up, mate!

The executive is a 30-year-old commercial officer who has been in the company for 3 years and has been promoted twice already. He holds a record for excellent sales performance and has shown willingness to support the company in an operational and strategic role, beyond his job description. I have been assigned to coach him, in order to support him in his new role, but also to help him stabilise mood swings that affect his morale, capacity for communication and energy levels (therefore a tendency for hypomanic episodes, if we want to look at it from a "clinical" perspective). As I had been involved with the company for a number of years and had known the executive from the first day he was hired, I was personally both engaged and motivated to contribute towards transforming "good" into "better". I also had a head start with regard to establishing rapport while, most importantly, being aware of the organisation's systemic parameters.

The first session rolled out easily, with both of us focusing on his rapid advancement, excellent customer relations and the innovative ideas he would like to bring into the department. I decided that recording strengths would suffice and decided to wait until the second session before moving matters forward, primarily in order to collect some first-hand data with regard to what was demotivating him, rather than to directly ask him.

A week later, I walked into the company and found the executive practically hidden behind his computer screen. It seemed as if he had not even realised I was there, despite me standing just a few metres away from him, and even though *Empathic Attunement* (a term first introduced by Heinz Kohut and defined as long-term empathic immersion by Rowe and Mac Isaac, 2000, p. 18) is not at the top of my coaching skills, I could practically touch the resentment, resistance and hostile introversion that dominated his existence. A few seconds later we were in the meeting room and I was trying to figure out exactly how this metamorphosis had taken place. After a brief outburst that mostly served to bring about relief rather than provide me with any valuable data, I was told that management was not receptive to his pioneering ideas, dismissed all proposals for new products and new markets, directly and indirectly undermined his authority over his team and minimised or did not recognise his achievements. Interestingly, the issue of remuneration was not once mentioned during the meeting. The executive threatened to leave. Challenges, conflicts and dilemmas kept running through my head like a shinkansen train. Some of the most prominent ones were:

* How can I motivate my coachee, when I have so little control over external/systemic circumstances?
* What is my position with regard to encouraging him or discouraging him to leave or stay in the company?
* Is it my place to discuss these symptoms with management during my next meeting with them, or should I not extend my coaching role to that of Organisational Development Consultant?

Coaching engagements, especially if you want to pursue excellence rather than stick to mechanistic methodologies, will often present you with such dilemmas and questions. The short answer to all of them is "it depends". At the same time and with regard to motivating your coachees, especially when things are not so straightforward, the following principles may come in handy:

* Promote *positive reframing* by utilising the concepts of Synchronicity (please see Chapter 5: Transformational leadership) and Adversity Activated Development (please see Chapter 8: Leading with PRAID).

- Construct an environment where *praise*, *appreciation* and celebration of *small victories* become a daily reality. Try to do so on an organisational level if your authority suffices.
- Suggest that your coachee takes accountability for *clear and clean information flow*: this will diminish paranoia and disengagement, which are major demotivators.
- Explore *values, goals* and *energy sources*, such as securing support from the environment and others.
- Clarify *meaning, direction* and *vision*.
- Most importantly, *lead your coachee by example* by displaying the capacity to self-motivate.

After a lot of hard work from all three sides (the coachee, management and myself) the executive has now been promoted to Commercial Director. Despite his natural tendency to protest and whine and the management's natural tendency to sabotage high-performing employees, he has displayed maturity and consistency; and increased his influence within and outside his company and role.

Engaging

Another way to categorise people: "I can", "I can't" and "I don't know" . . . who would *you* least want to work with?

Engagement has been the Holy Grail of HR departments practically forever; and rightly so. Retaining talent, securing commitment and benefiting from loyalty can make the difference, especially in times of turmoil. It is essential for the coach not only to secure their coachee's engagement, but also to help their coachee create circumstances for engagement for their team and people around them.

Historically, there has not been a single leader who had not secured the engagement of their people before moving on to achieve greatness, starting from Alexander the Great and Julius Caesar, moving on to Joan of Arc and Napoleon and more recently Gandhi and Che Guevara. You may have noticed that the majority of the people mentioned are part of military history. Even Gandhi's proposition to his people explicitly entailed a risk to their life. These are the people to take lessons from.

With regard to securing engagement from the coachee, in the event that their participation in the program is not entirely voluntary, your primary goal is to *create common ground and direction, clarify the benefits of the coaching process and achieve some early victories.* In addition and with regard to helping your coachee engage others, here is the short list of things to do:

- Invite them to elucidate and apprise those around them of the importance of their role.
- Help them create a sense of *solidarity*, *pride* and *belonging*. Some of this can be institutionalised through the establishment of social corporate events, corporate social responsibility (CSR) activities that involve everyone, corporate sports teams, etc. Make it up and help them make it up
- Encourage them to launch official and unofficial *praise and reward* schemes and mechanisms with integrity and fairness. It doesn't matter how big or small the team or the company: A solid succession plan for high achievers will give people the incentive they need to display the appropriate level of sportsmanship.
- Model a meaningful, caring and trusting coaching relation and help them reproduce it outside your session with others by identifying and establishing specific components that helped engagement levels. This will also be a good way of receiving feedback for your work.
- Convey to them that overpromising and under-delivering will eventually undermine their credibility.

Finally, I believe it is important to give your coachees permission to support themselves by not being constantly available, giving or overly generous due to fear of losing popularity and influence. It is a short-lived, inauthentic strategy and eventually they will pay for it. As Machiavelli puts it in *The Prince* (2007, p. 91 (translated from the Greek edition)): "And there is nothing that self depletes as much as generosity does; for by applying it, you lose the capacity to use it."

Transforming

Transformation and the processes surrounding it have already occupied one whole chapter of this text. However, it may be useful to place it within this more structured, prescriptive section, since this approach works better for some people. For a start, it is worth reminding ourselves that transformation is the counterproposal to change and not just immobility. This means that rather than render what has brought us this far "counterproductive" or "useless", we respectfully accept it as *having served its purpose and outlived its usefulness.* Therefore, rather than destroying something, we choose to develop it. This is an inclusive, humble approach, which also favours stability, since it enables us to work on existing foundations rather than resort to the radical "born-again-Christian" stance (or other born-again Persona), which is effectively a destructive approach. For coaching, this is particularly useful, since not only do you not have to reinvent the wheel, but you also have more available resources. What this means for coaches is that whether you originate from a psychology background, a business background, a finance background or any other, you will do well to honour and integrate this particular part of who you are into your coaching practice. For your clients, it means working with "what is" and with "who they are or can be" rather than trying to enforce your desire about them onto them. It is a fine balance and you will need to equip your internal supervisor well (please see Chapter 2: Coaching methodologies: "Supervision") in order to achieve it.

At the same time, transformation as a concept sits at the heart of coaching and begs the question as to whether coaching is a profession or a supplementary skill. I personally feel it is the latter and I would be very surprised, and perhaps disappointed, if at some point, executive coaching was offered primarily and exclusively at undergraduate level as an academic study rather than as a professional training. Coaching is something that offers you the opportunity to build on what you already have and on who you already are. It also requires a certain level of maturity (it is not a coincidence that most sport and other coaches are former "players"; it is rare that you see someone going straight into a coaching career). It is important that we keep this in mind and effectively convey it to our coachees.

One of the key aspects of transformation is Pace. The end of Chapter 8 will give us the opportunity to explore this further.

Chapter 8

Leading with PRAID
The evolution of leadership

Note: This chapter uses the terms "leader", "coachee" and "coach" inter-changeably, since it is the basic premise of this text that coaching is for leaders; and that a coach cannot coach and a leader cannot lead further than where they have been themselves.

> The seed of leadership grows in the soil of discipline, drinks from the water of valour and is warmed by the sun of victory.

I have just deleted well over 3,000 words; well over a quarter of this chapter. The same takes place with the equivalent Diploma module: It is heavily revised and transformed, consistently, year after year. After all, it has to do its title justice: this chapter is about the evolution of leadership and not about the golden-static-engraved-in-stone-principles of leadership.

Those of you who have paid close attention to what I have written to this point, must have clocked the importance and the competitive advantage that is to be gained, if one can *separate content from process*. We rarely change the way we do things, the process is more or less standardised, albeit subject to refinement. However, if we wish to succeed and thrive, we need to rely on and understand principles; and principles need to be content-based. Contrary to the major bulk of this text, therefore, this chapter (like the next one: Coaching for impact) is primarily about content: the content that makes a leader.

Over the past decade, I have drawn heavily from pioneers of coaching, such as Stephen Covey and Daniel Goleman; field strategists, such as Sun Tzu and Carl von Clausewitz; political animals, such as Niccolo Machiavelli and Gandhi; historical conquerors, such as Alexander the Great and Julius Caesar; business leaders, such as Henry Ford and Bill Gates; and probably a few *hundred* others, who have generously provided me with the foundation of *what a leader does, what a leader has and who a leader is*. This three-way segregation served for most of the time as the point of reference for the evolution of leadership. However useful this may have been for me and for trainees, I had not, until now, been able to integrate it into a model that had some kind of flow and sequence.

Two things lend themselves very well towards creating such a model. The first was the ever-increasing bulk and volume of work that I had to conduct both as a coach as well as an Organisational Development Consultant. My theoretical background was tried, tested, challenged and supported under real battle circumstances; and was, inevitably, transformed.

The second and most important parameter was the Greek crisis. Starting back in 2008, (and still going as this book is completing in 2017), the country's financial, business and social deficit called for focused, applicable, uncompromising delivery and method. It was fairly simple and straightforward: You had to achieve as much as possible, with as few resources as possible, within a minimum amount of time. Each and every assignment, coaching or organisational, explicitly or implicitly placed this demand upon me and the rest of Impact's team, never mind the client's team.

When the crisis struck Greece hard in 2008, it seemed that people had to step forward and take *accountability* for a positive outcome. In 2009 and 2010, a solid few years into the crisis, it appeared that only the *resilient* would make it to the other side. By 2012, accountability and resilience did not seem enough. Leaders had to consolidate, display patience, manage resources, organise themselves and others . . . a lot more. Any random, unplanned moves, any gambling could see an entire organisation to the end of its days. It was time to be *deliberate*. The last couple of years have shown some promise. Anybody who was not too busy making it to the next day, anybody who could see the future, anybody who had taken care to maintain relations, manage resources and secure access to information had the competitive advantage. The age of the *influencer* was dawning. The order, with which these characteristics come into action, may vary, depending on circumstances. However, there is one thing that remains unchanged, that remains central, that comes first and is vitally important: and that is *pace*. Out of the five leadership characteristics presented in this chapter, pace is the most difficult to define. The closest I can come to providing a one-off explanation is the following: *the ability and capacity to timely manage the urge for instant gratification, action or reaction, in a confident manner, as part of succeeding in greater objectives.*

The Greek crisis also meant that training and development budgets were significantly reduced. Coaching, following a global trend, became an excellent way to optimise performance. However, amateur coaches and "passers-by" could not and would not cut it any more and had to go home. Funds that had to be *utilised rather than spent*, and a blow to the competition, meant that the volume of projects reached unprecedented levels. So it was our turn to optimise the use of resources and time and become as effective as possible. It is at times like this that things come together, and what was once considered good enough is automatically rendered obsolete and replaced with an uncompromising pursuit of excellence. The model that follows is the tried-and-tested Adversity Activated Development distillation of this process, which has been successfully applied by several leaders

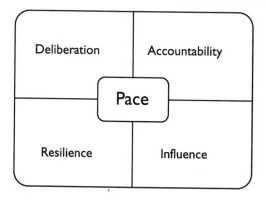

Figure 8.1 The PRAID Leadership Model

I have coached, over a decade of concrete crisis; and as such, portrays and presents the coach's developmental obligations towards their clients as well as themselves.

> Don't follow the road; don't even lead the way. *Pave* the way.

Deliberation

> There are three kinds of people: those who make things happen, those who watch what happens and those who protest about what happened.

Even though the PRAID model can be applied in any sequence, I am choosing to kick off with *Deliberation*, for two reasons. First of all, it is a provocative term

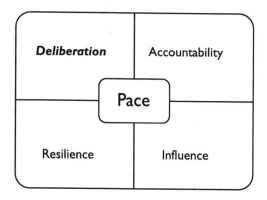

Figure 8.2 The PRAID Leadership Model – Deliberation

(my mentors would reframe and replace the word with "evocative", but I do have to be true to my own, authentic sentiment). Second, coaching is all about aligning intention and outcome; and one can only be deliberate in doing so.

In our collective mind, deliberation alludes to Machiavellian thinking, propaganda, politics, lobbying and more. All "immoral" words. When asked to account for the factors that stop them from being the best they can, usually during the chemistry meeting (at times also referred to as the scouting meeting), approximately half of the executives I work with indicate that others are better "at promoting themselves". This is somehow meant to show me that their progression and success are not related to their skills and capacity; it is meant to show me that other people's progression and success are not related to their skills and capacity; it is meant to show me that it's *"unfair"* and that there is a moral high ground to be occupied by not being deliberate – and consequently, by *sacrificing influence.*

It shows me nothing other than lack of vision and focus, an impaired ability to engage and toil in strategising; and *if you can't be deliberate about your own progression, why should anyone trust you in undertaking such a task for their company?*

The same goes for the coaches themselves. If you and your client don't clarify the actual objective of your collaboration or, if needed, you don't guide your client towards identifying their objectives, with transparency or even audacity, then you will most likely be wasting each other's time or at least colluding in underperforming. Executive coaching is about improving performance; unleashing potential; it is about, yes, we can. And if I wanted to use dirty, politically incorrect, frowned-upon terminology at this stage, it is about *winning, not whining.*

Let's look at the definition of deliberation:

> 1. *careful consideration before decision.*
> 2. *formal consultation or discussion.*
> 3. *deliberate quality; leisureliness of movement or action;* . . . .

(www.dictionary.com)

I particularly like the use of the term "leisure" in this definition. It indicates that after careful consideration, you can set and determine the pace, as opposed to being *subjected*, a rather passive position to find yourself in, to the pace of other people or circumstances outside your control.

At the end of the day, deliberation is all about strategy. It is about deciding "what you want to be when you grow up" (an intervention that I frequently address to my clients), it is about aligning your actions and behaviours (tactics) with the "end game". And as a coach, you need to be in a position to proactively, fearlessly and shamelessly convey this to your coachee.

But how do you go about achieving the above? In my opinion, there are three key areas that a coach must dig into first. The first one is the client's *Vision* (about themselves, their team, their company, etc.). The second is the way with which they maintain their team's *Formation Alignment* (the assumption being that most

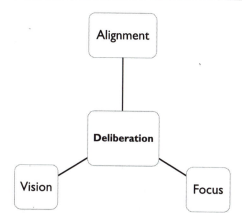

Figure 8.3 Deliberation components

of the executives you will work with are actually team leaders). Finally, it is about the ability to maintain *Focus*.

Vision

> ˙Don't let the things you don't want cloud the view of the things you want . . .

Seneca the Younger (first century AD, Letter LXXI, line 3) apparently once said, "If you don't know which port you are sailing to, no wind is favourable". A couple of thousand years later, Stephen Covey (1989, p. 95) subscribed to and prescribed, "Begin with the end in mind". It is to be hoped that, as coaches, we all have our vision. Mine is to bring about transformation in the business world, directly by coaching leaders and indirectly by training them via the Diploma. I call it the evolution of leadership and you are reading all about it right here, right now. No, actually, I am doing something about actualising it right now, by writing this text on a Sunday evening, a few minutes before midnight just ahead of a Monday that contains an 8-hour workshop for a multinational, a meeting to discuss project prospects at a financial institution straight after and a business dinner with one of the Diploma facilitators to discuss expansion strategy. *What is your vision and what do you need to give up and prioritise to achieve it?*

The place to start with vision is to invite your client to *articulate* it and, if necessary, to write it down. Mumbling aimlessly for a few minutes won't cut it. It needs to be contained within a sentence. Second, it is important to check the *intention* behind the vision, since every "what" must be accompanied by a "why". Securing sponsors, supporters and even *people* to delegate to is the next point on our list and the transition point towards Formation Alignment.

The above should keep you busy for several sessions. On occasion, provided that the vision is missing or dated, you may kick off your collaboration by searching for it. It is hygienic, useful and strategic, and creates opportunity for rapport, alliance and overall alignment.

Formation Alignment

> Group performance is determined decisively by its least effective members. Develop them, fire them, reallocate them; but do something; now.

Formation Alignment describes the phenomenon whereby a team's *direction*, *purpose* and *aspiration* are mutual and aligned. It is the leader's job (your client, that is) to achieve this, usually with the help of an external consultant (executive coach or Organisational Development Consultant, that's you). Invite your coachee to assess whether their team members, supporters, sponsors, and perhaps even people in their life, are aligned under similar *principles*, working towards achieving the same *mission*, that they have complimentary *expertise* and that there are no *extreme bottom outliers*. Top outliers are fine, since they can push the team forward – unless they deviate in other ways, which can also prove costly, such as taking too many risks, or trying to "capture the flag" all by themselves. Those in the middle are also OK.

If we wanted to become even more Machiavellian and deliberate in our thinking and intervention, then we could even invite our client to consider or envisage how their intervention with regard to bottom outliers could inspire or set an example for others. Whatever the case, they need to take action, since teams and human nature overall have tendencies to follow gravity.

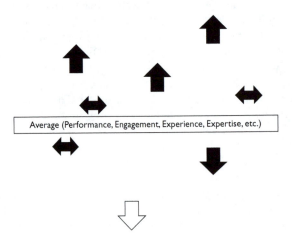

Figure 8.4 Outliers: Leaders need to address the issue; proactively and with deliberation

It is my personal opinion that Formation Alignment ought to be enforced with regard to *engagement* or even *performance*. Several people find this approach somewhat absolutist, since I am indirectly advocating getting rid of the bottom outlier. Alexander the Great most certainly would. Imagine a Macedonian phalanx in which a couple of soldiers decided they would go slower than the rest, or simply could not keep up with the rest of the formation. It would not really support the Greek leader's vision of conquering the known world now, would it? Whatever the case, it is vital that your coachee has some understanding of who the bottom outliers are on their team, the impact this has on collective performance and the impact certain interventions would bring about.

Case Study 11: Better you, than everyone else

The coachee is a senior executive in the pharmaceutical industry and has actually arranged to meet me on her own initiative (rather than have the HR department find her a coach). She has been referred by a client in another pharmaceutical company and has indicated that the company has agreed to fund her coaching sessions, regardless. She indicates that despite leading a very competent team of six Category Heads of Sales (she is the company's Commercial Director), two of them are never able to reach their target. Since it is virtually impossible to interview six people as well as their teams of five to ten sales reps, we decide to devise a semi-structured interview that she will be conducting with her six members of staff. The intention is to identify discrepancies in individual performance, engagement and motivation. The interview is deliberately designed to introduce a number of topics so that it will not appear as if there is an element of assessment. The design of the interview takes a couple of sessions, during which time she provides me with very useful information with regard to how certain sales reps are always protesting, very openly and very loudly, about their career advancement. I also pick up that a couple of Category Heads are particularly conflict-averse as well as unable to hold their members of staff accountable for their performance and results. Unsurprisingly, they all happen to inhabit the same two categories. When asked what she had done about this situation, my coachee indicated that they had all been there for such a long time and it had not crossed her mind to challenge them. The rest of our work consisted of coaching her to manage conflict as well as the restructuring of the whole organisational chart; which consisted of mixing and matching people in a way that would enable top performers to monitor and influence bottom performers. In addition, she decided to remove one of the Category Heads. Sometimes, we can't afford the opportunity cost of Formation Misalignment. It's like one bad fruit in a basket of many good ones.

Focus

During my coaching career, I have encountered a number of executives who had trouble sticking to deadlines, making difficult decisions and organising their time and resources. Some were aware that this decreased their chances of success; some wore the "creative and untamed" hat as a badge of honour; a few were simply lazy. Given that your coachee knows where they want to go (vision), you should be able to help them focus in getting there.

The following are some fundamental considerations that you may wish to introduce to your work:

- *Distinguish* between *activity* and *achievement.*
- *Measure* twice – *cut* once (Stephen Covey's "Sharpen the saw"; 1989, p. 287).
- *Win the war,* not the battle: *Tactical* retreat is an option.
- *Prioritise.*
- *Develop* personal and professional *values* (similar to what this chapter means to me).

Having helped your client establish their Vision, optimise their team's alignment and generate focus, it is time to move to proactive action. Accountably.

Accountability

Criticism should stop being out of bounds; criticise others and yourself not for not being good enough but into being as great as you can be.

The ability to see things through is probably what distinguishes leaders from the rest of the people. It's called *accountability* and my definition of it is *the art and*

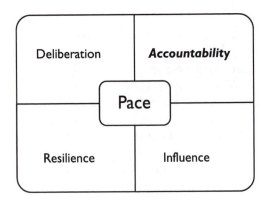

Figure 8.5 The PRAID Leadership Model – Accountability

act of undertaking to successfully lead and deliver an assigned or unassigned objective. Some people confuse it with the concept of responsibility. It is not to be confused so lightly. Responsibility usually refers to past actions, very often unsuccessful ones, hence the accusatory "Who is responsible for this?" or the brave, yet mostly useless "I am willing to take full responsibility" that usually follows a mess.

Stephen R. Covey and Stephen M.R. Covey deliver two poignant insights that describe the difference between responsibility and accountability in a rather succinct way.

Stephen R. Covey: *You can't talk yourself out of a problem you've behaved yourself into.*

Stephen M.R. Covey: *No, but you can behave yourself out of a problem that you've behaved yourself into . . . and often faster than you think.*

(Covey, S.M.R. [with Merrill], 2006, p. 127)

I often encapsulate the "dialogue" above when exploring the concept of failure with associates, clients or colleagues by indicating that *I don't care much about why you couldn't make it happen, yet I am more than happy to explore how we will.*

Whether I am working in the context of Organisational Development (i.e., with teams) or in the context of executive coaching (i.e., with individuals), I very frequently invite my clients to step forward and commit to carrying themselves or their organisation to the next level. No excuses, just a plain and simple commitment, supported with *valour, good planning, risk management and realistic expectations.*

The primary ingredient in being able to deliver is discipline; and I have yet to meet an executive whose lack of *discipline* did not interfere negatively with their plans and deliberations.

There is a simple methodology in tackling the issue of discipline and it originates primarily from the *project management* discipline (pun intended). If it is merely a result of poor organisation, lack of skills, project management expertise, etc., then you can support your client by inviting them to address the five parameters presented at the end of this section for themselves and/or for their team: In addition, it is worth exploring the *allocation of resources.* This methodology, combined with periodic follow-up (in essence and as indicated, a basic project management methodology), should see deliberations accomplished. If this approach does not work, then don't worry, the exercise has not been in vain: Instead, *it has served as a diagnostic tool* in identifying what the lack of discipline is actually a *symptom* of. (For more on symptoms, please see Chapter 5: Transformational leadership). The findings may reveal lack of engagement, lack of expertise, poor recruiting, problematic team dynamics, unclear Vision, mission or objectives and more. Whatever is the case, you will have facilitated your client's organisational and/or

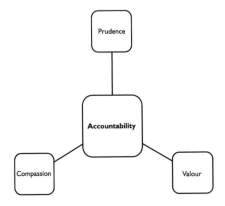

Figure 8.6 Accountability components

individual diagnosis and consequently enhanced their awareness of the situation. The checklist that follows is a useful aid in coaching accountable leaders:

- Your commitment pertains to the future.
- The delivery point in time is more (preferably) or less defined and a deadline applies.
- You have transparently clarified the use of resources (human and other) your objective requires.
- You have considered and presented the desired strategic and other impact that successful completion will have for individuals as well as for the whole.
- You are willing to assume responsibility, should the project fail, without looking for scapegoats.

Please read this list carefully and consider how frequently the aforementioned criteria are being fulfilled. Now consider the impact that their fulfilment would have on the efficiency, productivity and overall success of your clients.

Prudence

Once this step has been achieved, it is time to equip them with *prudence*. Prudence, in essence, is nothing other than basic project management methodology and consists of defining the parameters below:

- Priorities (What)
- Delegation (Who)
- Organisation (How)
- Time–Space (When–Where)
- Resources (time, skills, expertise, data, influence, money, etc.)

If these parameters have been addressed with clarity, then individuals and organisations supported by you will have gained a monumental head start. A fundamental aspect of supporting prudence is to invite your clients (whether individual in the context of coaching or a group in the context of OD) to wrap up all calls to action with the above checklist. Similar to the procedure I presented in Chapter 6 (Systems-focused executive coaching), it is often the simplest of methods that can provide us with a head start towards success. When sharing such approaches, I half jokingly indicate that in terms of generating work volume for myself, it is often a bad idea, since it can cut an engagement in half.

Compassion

An accountable leader shows *compassion*. Admittedly, being somewhat challenged in the empathy department, I find my own guideline fairly hard to follow. I am a harsh critic; however, I have been fortunate enough to have my work monitored and supervised by highly empathic mentors. This includes my Aikido (Japanese martial art) teacher who from time to time hands over the class to me and always tells me off at the end for giving beginners a hard time and expecting them to display the kind of accuracy and precision that an experienced martial artist would possess. I know that some of you understand exactly where I come from and some others are baffled at such unreasonableness and lack of sympathy. Both are right: There is a limit to how much we can interfere with our nature. Nonetheless, the first thing to do if you suspect that you are not particularly compassionate (or not particularly empathic), is to ask people who are close to you to point out when you are being somewhat insensitive or unaccommodating.

Empathy is a primary tool in sensing, experiencing and displaying compassion and we have touched upon it in Chapter 4: Fundamental skills: "Generating data": "Projective Identification". However, compassion stems beyond empathy in that it mobilises our willingness to be accountable and help; and this is a key attribute both for coaches as well as leaders. In addition to modelling a compassionate relation (which should, of course, stop well before we endorse our coachee's learned helplessness, perhaps to validate our own narcissistic, rescuer needs; and yes, please do read this sentence one more time), we should enable our clients to comprehend and reflect on the following:

How can I help?

Especially with clients who lead teams or organisations and are fairly aloof, isolated, lacking in empathy and protesting about how little they get from others (thus assuming a victim's or persecutor's position), you should prescribe that they try asking this question once or twice a week, *preferably to the same person to start with*; and then observe the shift in the relation, provided they are willing to deliver on their offer. It is a bold experiment; however, one that can have a great return if conducted full heartedly. You should also support your client's understanding of the following:

- Being compassionate creates opportunity for contact, synergy and exchange of information, which can lead to innovation, influence and optimisation of resources.
- Engagement and motivation are key aspects for high-performance delivery. Leaders who show no interest in the well-being of their teams, do not recognise their efforts and do not verbalise appreciation, risk jeopardising it.

Relations are rendered sustainable only through reciprocity. No one, especially in the corporate context, is altruistic enough to give without taking. If a leader gives, they should expect to receive. This should also stop them from complaining about having to do everything all by themselves. Unless they need to complain; in which case, a coach needs to explore the purpose this serves (please see Chapter 9: Coaching for impact: "What purpose does this serve?")

Valour

> To support people's evolution, hold them accountable for it; to win popularity contests, assent that others are responsible for its standstill.

I have only recently added *valour* to my list of key leadership characteristics. Not because I only recently realised its importance or started believing in it; but because I subconsciously feared the mockery and dismissal that such a trait would receive in our day and age. However, as time went by and I completed more and more projects, I realised that there are still executives out there who will bravely take risks, stand up for their values and principles and protect others. Such a stance comes at a cost; however, there are also benefits and you should explore those with your client, especially if they appear to be intimidated, cornered and lacking in initiative; in other words, if they fear assuming accountability (or even standing up for what they believe). Below are my thoughts regarding valour, since it is not a quality I can possibly, methodologically, prescribe.

- I try to avoid the integration of existential components in executive coaching to the best of my ability; however, *how long can you hide who you are behind your finger?* Worse yet, *how long can you go on without exploring and at least partly finding out who you are?* The text has addressed such issues in previous sections, such as the *Persona* and *authenticity* (please see Chapter 5: Transformational leadership; and Chapter 9: Coaching for impact).
- Being governed by *fear* and/or *avoidance* is not only a short-lived strategy that will eventually lead to an escalated conflict. It is also a guarantee that your

client (or your client's team members) will take every opportunity to resist or display passive aggression, through lack of cooperation, minimum contribution, "forgetfulness" and several other performance cutbacks. Encourage them to talk straight and persistently explore how they compensate for their lack of valour through other, potentially counterproductive, behaviour.

- It takes valour to not be avoidant and *separate content from process* as well as to *explore cause and purpose rather than stick to symptoms* (please see Chapter 4: Fundamental skills; and Chapter 5: Transformational leadership). The corporate world is not used to such challenges. Troubleshooting prevails and, more often than not, leaders deal with the problem at hand instead of taking advantage to understand organisational and individual processes better. Try to share this decoding wisdom with your coachee, primarily by modelling it within the coaching relation. Some key interventions in achieving this are the following: "What is *really* going on here?" as well as "There seems to be a prevailing/repeated *theme* here" and finally, "What *purpose* does this serve?" This will gradually alert them and draw their attention to what is actually strategically important (and is perhaps being avoided) rather than what seems to be tactically important. '

- The art of giving and receiving *feedback* has been covered extensively in this text. It will come as no surprise that until you and your clients get used to it, it will appear as a Herculean task. It is not easy to share your thoughts about someone with that person and it may be even more difficult to ask them to share theirs about you. Modelling this behaviour within the coaching relation will enable your client to try it outside, in the "real" world. If necessary, start them off with easy steps and build it up. Good pace, to be further explored at the end of this chapter, is of the essence.

Influence

Influence, nowadays, is not about self-importance or authority; it is about self-awareness and quality relations.

Carpenters have tape measures and chisels, blacksmiths have hammers and nippers and coaches have *influence*. And so should their coachees and all leaders in general. It is important to comprehend that this is also, in one way or another, the underlying request that our clients place on us: whether they are being coached to improve their time management, finetune how they relate to others, motivate their team or improve their negotiation skills, the *ability and capacity to deliberately determine, direct and increase the transformational impact* they have on people and circumstances is key. It would, therefore, be sensible to deduce that in addition to drawing their attention to the four pillars of influence, as they will be addressed in this chapter, we need to display and model these very elements ourselves in an uncompromised yet authentic fashion.

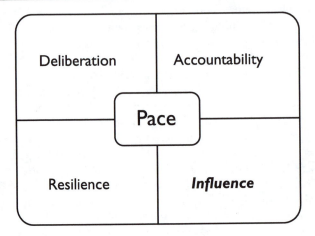

Figure 8.7 The PRAID Leadership Model – Influence

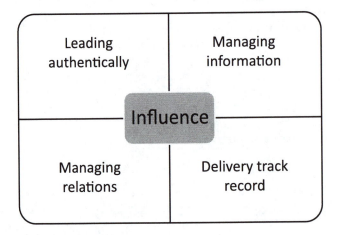

Figure 8.8 Influence

Leading authentically

There is a plethora of literature on leadership out there, which for the most part focuses on the Persona of the great leader, in a more or less directive way. I am a big fan of this literature and have spent a fair amount of time extracting lessons from the achievements and traits of the likes of Alexander the Great, Sun Tzu and Clausewitz, to name a few. At the same time, I am not averse to the risky notion of "fake it until you make it" and "dress for the job you want, not the one you currently hold". After all, we need to maintain a forward momentum, we need to practically *blackmail* ourselves into a forward momentum. And generating expectation from and for others, and ourselves, is a fine way to achieve this.

At the same time, as our experience, authority and seniority level rise, we become more visible and we need not just to display, but also to own a steady footing. People who receive executive coaching services are usually senior and seniority requires that they gain a solid understanding not just of who they want to be, but also of who they are. Self-awareness is clearly a fundamental prerequisite and understanding the balance between the Persona and the Authentic Self can be a great asset. A big discrepancy between the internal sentiment and the external expression will usually result in *pseudocompetence* (Clarkson, 1994) and will seriously compromise our client's ability to *lead authentically*.

What does pseudocompetence look like though?

Have you ever sat down with a client who has an answer, an explanation, a theory or an alternative for every proposal, feedback or intervention that comes from your side? To the extent that it makes you wonder why they opted to be coached in the first place? And makes you (and chances are, others around them as well) want to just get up and leave; because you just don't see the point, or feel you have nothing to offer (which is a fine case of Projective Identification, by the way; please see Chapter 4: Fundamental skills: "Psychodynamic competencies and the use of self"). Congratulations, chances are that you have just come across the Archetype of a pseudocompetent executive. Knowing and being able to do everything and never asking for help are their trademark behaviours; which is clearly the combined outcome of self-depreciation – that is, "if others really knew how incompetent I am, then I would lose everything" – and resistance or even fear of change. Some people can manage to live their whole lives like this without anybody ever finding out. However, even if this is the case, the anxiety that accompanies pseudocompetence is enough reason to want to do something about it. This "something" entails some serious work from the side of the coach that will drive them towards supporting what they do with who they are, as indicated earlier (Chapter 1) in the section "Who can become an executive coach".

Let's explore the coach's options, when working with their client's capacity and ability to lead authentically:

1   Invite your client to support themselves (please see Chapter 3: Presence: "Rapport").
2   Initiate your client into the concept of feedback (please see Chapter 4: Fundamental skills: "Giving and receiving feedback").
3   Support them in "getting it wrong". It may be useful to assign them a task that they will likely fail at (best to keep clear of something crucial, dangerous or unethical here).
4   Pseudocompetence can be expressed through extreme compliance, whereby the individual adjusts to any situation like a chameleon; or through extreme reaction, whereby the individual is opinionated and rigid. Identify the polarity (please see Chapter 5: Transformational leadership) and experiment in generating some meaning.

5   Introduce the concept of the Persona; and synergise with your client in discovering the balance between being and doing (please see Chapter 5: Transformational leadership).
6   Needless to say, lead by example. If you do not model all of the above behaviours yourself, just talking about them will simply not cut it.

It is important to comprehend that supporting your client's battle against pseudo-competence does not under any circumstances mean neglecting the importance of the image they adopt for the world. I do not know of one leader who did not attend to their *presence and presentation* (the Persona, that is) in one way or another.

There is no doubt that your client's projected Persona has won them some battles and lost them others. Coaching should see it turn to an asset and an ally. This is more complicated than choosing the right suit and wearing the right watch. It is a question of attitude, and a winning attitude is most frequently an authentic one that *integrates as many components of who we are as possible, with minimum effort; including* the quirky or weird ones, which may even turn into a trademark (another element that has historically been tactically utilised by leaders, especially during times of war, in order to, for example, like the Red Baron, inspire troops or intimidate the enemy). It is important that this process is supported in a natural way and propels forward existing characteristics. You can't take a man or woman who enjoys luxury, space and comfort and put them in a pair of ripped, tight jeans and a rusty, old Beetle car and expect they will behave naturally, just because they work in a youngish, hip, IT company. In addition, the most rewarding aspect of this "study" may actually come whilst exploring with your client who they are naturally inclined to be. Collecting feedback, with regard to the impact that their presence and presentation have on others, is, needless to say, essential. Your own freedom and inclination as a coach to take risks, to be your authentic self, will act as permission for your client to follow your example. Build it up as your experience increases. With valour.

Managing information

Knowledge is power and influential leaders (and this includes coaches themselves) need to have access to it. Knowledge stems beyond accumulating expertise, reading books or extracting information from search engines. It extends to gaining access to information (including opinions, feedback, feelings, etc.) that is not available to other people.

According to Sun Tzu in his iconic text, *The Art of War*: "If we know that our men are in a position to attack, but are unaware that the enemy is not open to attack, we have only gone half way through victory" (cited by Clavell, 1981, p. 67).

Data collection can take place in a very structured, almost ritualistic manner. Invite your client to *schedule* weekly meetings with their associates or their team, with the sole aim being the exchange of information; invite them to make a point of receiving *feedback* from at least one person every week or from the same person every week concerning their individual progress on a specific task or skill; invite them to standardise some type of *newsletter* for associates or colleagues. Above all, though, invite them to sharpen up their ability to perceive and display empathy (to be addressed in the very next section), for these are the primary skills that give us access to data and support our capacity to influence.

Wikipedia (2017, n. p.) defines perception as "the organisation, identification, and interpretation of sensory information in order to represent and understand the environment". This has got to be without any question an ongoing, rigorous, deliberate, conscious and unconscious process that leads to *intelligence* (which is the synonym used for data-collecting agencies and not without reason). Leaders should be in a position to collect verbal and non-verbal data, hard and soft data, process and content data, connect the dots, identify (past and present) patterns and put it all to good use in order to be able to influence the circumstances and future for themselves, their team and their organisation. The ability to collect data constitutes one of the coach's key assets and this is one area, where the coach, in addition to modelling, should feel free to act as a mentor for their client and practically teach them how to do it. Chapter 4 (Fundamental skills: "Generating data") can provide a useful aid.

Having supported your client's ability to collect information, it is time to help them to distribute information. The distribution of information, be it feedback, news, future plans, etc., needs to take place in a way that is aligned with your client's strategic goals (and, it is hoped, for the benefit of those they lead). Leaders should filter the information they distribute in a way that proliferates their positions and interests; supports individual, collective and strategic objectives; and generates engagement and motivation. If it sounds propagandistic, Machiavellian, almost Goebbels-esque, well, it's because it is. No more than advertising and branding, though. *Prescribing* that they read Machiavelli should be top of your list on the things to do with and for them, by the way.

Managing relations

We are not just what we know; we are also *who* we know and relate to. The influence that you have on the network of people around you will determine how well your messages will be amplified, and will provide you with the shortest and most effective possible route to achieving your objectives. Managing relations does not have to look or be the same for everyone. For example, introverts (to use a rather broad classification system) will find it easier to have fewer, more intimate relations. Extroverts can benefit from a phone book the size of *The Encyclopaedia Britannica*. You should encourage your client to pursue a relational model that authentically matches their character and personality. At the same time, you should challenge the notion that networking, relating and interacting are merely "political" means for getting to where you want to go without putting in the work or possessing the talent. Integrating both is a potent combination and such introjects are usually used as an excuse for or protest against the inability to secure influence. Let's therefore explore how you can support your client's influence by helping them optimise the way they relate.

The first place to visit, whilst connecting with people, especially in the business world, is *reciprocity*, which Stephen Covey successfully coined as *"win–win"* (1989). The term "mutual benefit" may bring to mind Mafia networks; however, the fact that this was used for the wrong purpose does not mean that it was the wrong method. It is worth considering what the other person will gain from liaising with you and more often than not, it is advisable to give before expecting to receive. A sense of entitlement, lack of generosity or an arrogant attitude can prove very costly, in the middle to long term. Convey this to your client and invite them to explore the extent to which their relations are reciprocal, the extent to which they are of use (or even indispensable) to others and the frequency with which they contact others to provide help rather than to be facilitated. It may be worth prescribing that your client strategically helps one select person per day, without being asked.

Which brings us to *strategic alliances*. In the context of strategic, utilitarian, deliberation, your clients need to learn to distribute their time and effort, in a way that prioritises interaction with *key players*. Key players are not necessarily those who hold the highest positions, make the most money or display a snobbish attitude. *Key players are those people who display PRAID characteristics.* Go through a list of major players who surround them (or you for that matter) and assess how they can prove useful in the next 2 to 5 years. Devise a communication and relation strategy that will strengthen your client's standing in relation to key players and, of course, carefully examine how these relations can be *reciprocal* and *mutually beneficial*. Assess which people are a waste of space and time in your client's sphere. You might get some of them wrong. That's OK. The opportunity cost of sustaining relations with parasitic individuals is simply way too high. You can't just maintain useless relations just because one day these individuals may surprise you. That's a Polyanna-type approach for random, and not deliberate, leaders. Provide them with a sense of confidence and work away feelings of guilt and insecurity. This will optimise their influence opportunity cost.

Daniel Goleman marked "recognising emotions in others" (1995, p. 47) as one of the top five domains for emotional intelligence. He was referring to *empathy*, and in the business world, there is no doubt in my mind, it is an absolute prerequisite for influence.

He went on to describe people who cannot experience it as "emotionally tone-deaf" (1995, p. 47). For one reason or another, certain people possess and develop a much higher degree of emotional empathy, which, depending on how they utilise it, can do them and others service or disservice. It is important to clarify that not everyone is equally empathic, and even though empathy can be developed in some cases, our natural predisposition and developmental history have the final say. There are several theories out there and even more "should" and "should not" positions, and you are welcome to explore them further for yourself.

However, it is unlikely that you do not have some idea regarding your capacity to empathically relate.

Psychopathology and mental disorders aside, if your client can pick up other people's emotions physically to the extent that they generate an emotional and bodily disturbance, then they are on one end of the spectrum. If discovering that people close and around them are unwell or have been unwell hits your client as a surprise, then they inhabit the other end of the scale; and then of course, there are all the in-betweens, which most of us occupy. In the event that your client (or you even) are not the most empathic creature on earth, the good news is that you can rely on *cognitive empathy*. Cognitive empathy is nothing more and nothing less than *the ability to employ perception and observation to extract meaningful data*. This may involve staying sharply focused to observe subtle or less subtle changes in your client's overall demeanour and behaviour, observing the fluctuation in their use of language or simply asking them, to find out how they are. It is all in the context of relating, managing information and increasing our influence.

How does empathy (natural or cognitive) contribute towards increasing our influence, then?

Caring enough to know where the other person is, emotionally, greatly improves the quality of a *relation*; collecting *intelligence* about the other's state of being increases the chances of generating timely synergies; assessing who is most fit to perform certain tasks under certain circumstances utilises, secures and filters the best possible *resources*.

In addition to helping your coachee sharpen up their capacity to *display* empathy, your job is also to help them calibrate it. Too much, and they are bound to be swayed left, right and centre to save the world, ending up drained and sapped, so help them take a step back; too little, and people will struggle to connect with them, so help them build on their (cognitive) empathy. Needless to say, it is important that we address the issue for ourselves, be it with our own coach, therapist or supervisor.

Having looked at how to enhance our ability to relate in this section, we will also be exploring ways in which we jeopardise and sabotage closeness. Chapter 9 will address ways in which we regulate distance from others ("How do you lose and gain influence?").

Delivery Trust Record

> Make competition your friend; pick out the best and uncompromisingly, restlessly, relentlessly push yourself to surpass them.

In a functional, fair, meritocratic work environment and in addition to leading by example, it is our delivery track record that inspires confidence and trust in others. Stephen M.R. Covey could not have put it better, when he wrote, "The counterfeit is delivering activities instead of results" (2006, p. 172). Our historical success, achievement and efficacy determine and define our *Delivery Trust Record*; and dramatically increase our capacity to influence.

Integrity, *worth* and *consistency* have to be modelled by the coach, prior to exploring their significance with the coachee. This means that before preaching and advising, you have to walk the talk. This entails displaying loyalty, punctuality, engagement, dependable performance and overall reliability. I call this process *earning and spending trust credit and debit*. The system works in a way similar to banking: If you place your cash in a time deposit and leave it there for some time, the bank will reward you with an interest of a couple of percentile points (even less at the moment, a period of significant lack of trust globally), depending on a number of factors. However, borrowing money (e.g., through credit cards, debit accounts, mortgages, etc.) will see you paying back your debt with a much higher interest (for example, the credit card interest rate at the moment sits at around 15% plus). It's the same with trust credit and debit. It will only take one wrong step to undo the good work and credit you have painstakingly accumulated. You need to understand this; and so do your coaching clients. This is the connecting principle behind accountability and influence: If you volunteer to get things done and repeatedly do so, your influence will increase. Correspondingly, as Harris Kern put it: "Committing to something and then not following through, is the surest way to wreck your integrity instantaneously" (2003, p. 46).

As indicated, it is vital to distinguish between *responsibility* and *accountability*. We usually assume responsibility for something that has gone wrong (and less often right) in the past. Apologising is the epitome of that. Some people argue that apologising is a good thing. It might be. I don't see it that way, at least not to the extent that others do. Personally, if someone wronged me or got something wrong in relation to me, I would much prefer it if they took accountability for fixing it or invited me to co-generate a solution. Personally, I also give people far less credit for assuming responsibility than most do. I much prefer it when they say, "*I will be* responsible for that", even though what they mean is, "I will be accountable for that". It does not really matter what they say. What matters is what they do. This is why I feel *apologising is overrated; especially by comparison to a positive trust record of delivery*. This is the reason that people with a poor delivery record have little or no influence over me, regardless of whether they assume responsibility or not, and as a matter of fact, *regardless of their intention*. I appreciate this may seem harsh; it is, however, also a fact, both in business and in life.

Our Delivery Trust Record, therefore, effectively depends on our success rate of assuming accountability. Every time we fail to deliver, we move from being an accountable individual to becoming a responsible individual (unless we shy away from that also, which then renders us completely unreliable or a sociopath, even).

The Delivery Trust Record formula that determines influence looks something like this:

Assumption of Accountability + Successful Delivery + Trust Record = + Influence

The formula that usually leads to assuming responsibility and decreases influence is:

Assumption of Accountability + Unsuccessful Delivery - Trust Record = - Influence

Resilience

Rejoice! Depending on who *they* are, your judges and critics may be the confirmation that you are doing something right.

Regardless of how competent, intelligent, skilled, strategic, methodical, deliberate or influential we are, we will from time to time *fail*. This book has made no secret about the fact that the – recent – glorification of failure and the mediocrity it promotes is outside any coaching or leadership context. At the same time, failure and disappointment, due to our own shortcomings – or, less frequently, misfortune, as a result of circumstance – are inevitable stages in life and business; and unless you equip yourself in dealing with them, you won't be getting very far. For coaches, being able to manage failure and disappointment is vitally important, since our clients will very often come to us during challenging, difficult times; and they don't just want us to provide them with an one-off solution: They need us to equip them with the capacity to overcome and eventually utilise obstacles, challenges and blockages; and even then, we might not be able to get it right, as most of the case studies in this text choose to illustrate, instead of serving up a bunch of textbook success stories. Perhaps they even need us to help them be the last man or woman standing. At the end of the day, they need our support in building *resilience*.

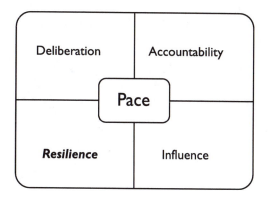

Figure 8.9 The PRAID Leadership Model – Resilience

Figure 8.10 Resilience

Adversity Activated Development

If you have read this far, then you have already come across Renos Papadopoulos, my supervisor, mentor and colleague, who, together with Jung, is responsible for the theory around transformational leadership (Chapter 5). After working extensively with refugees, through various international organisations, such as the United Nations High Commissioner for Refugees (UNHCR), Renos discovered that the caretaker's disposition often directed the refugee towards a victim role. He rightly deduced that a victim role led to victim behaviour, which would under no circumstances equip refugees with what they needed to rebuild their lives. Furthermore, and more importantly though, Renos realised that these people had access to an arsenal of experience and expertise that the rest of us didn't; and that this actually provided them with a competitive advantage over everyone else (Papadopoulos, 2007). The key to unlocking this potential did not just lie in letting caretakers – and the rest of the world – know that this was the case, so that they would shift their behaviour. The key, primarily, lay in working with the refugees to shift their self-perception. He named the fundamental theoretical position behind this *Adversity Activated Development (AAD)*; and as a coach, it has so far served me in helping hundreds of coachees, executives and students metamorphose from a protesting, sulking, disabled victim into a competitive, ambitious, transfigured leader.

In terms of practically applying this sort of intervention for executive coaching, I rely on the factors below, which are for the most part cognitive:

1   What do you now know, possess, understand which you did not before?
2   How does that give you an advantage over your former self?
3   How does that give you an advantage over others?
4   How do you feel this adversity will support a new direction for you?

For me, the answers that I receive to these questions (for example, from an executive who has been bypassed for promotion for the third time) also show me what the individual is "made of", for even with all the coaching in the world, I believe that some core aspects remain unchanged. The key is to support the executive in looking inwards towards themselves, rather than outwards towards others. If you feel that everyone, except yourself, determines your destiny, then you have very little control over it.

On occasion, and if I sense that the coachee is determined to occupy a victim position and that the opportunity cost of working with them (instead of helping someone else, for example) is too high, I will abort the mission altogether. There is a limit to how much resilience one wants to build after a certain stage, especially if you can pick and choose. Nonetheless, during the early days of my career, and this goes for everyone just entering the profession, being forced to work with impossible cases, due to limited choice, is truly what will take your practice to the next level; provided that you find a supervisor who will help you metabolise your disappointment to productivity – someone like Renos Papadopoulos, who has also supported the material around conflict below.

Utilising conflict

Building resilience greatly depends on surviving, managing and eventually utilising *conflict*. Conflict takes place on an individual (intrapsychic), dyadic and collective scale, almost reflecting a parallel process (please see Chapter 4: Fundamental skills: "Generating data": "Parallel process"). For our coachees, adversity comes in the form of defeat in their battles against other parties or in the form of unresolved, internal polarities. More often than not, our external conflict is a natural, reflective continuation and manifestation of our internal clashes. It is worth keeping that in mind when coaching; however, it is advisable to be careful with relevant interventions, at least until you accumulate some mileage, and certainly whilst engaged in solid supervision. (The section "Epistemology–Position–Action" in Chapter 5 can further support your understanding of how our belief system determines our behaviour). What you can, however, work with, which would also nicely match your AAD framework, is the choice that your coachee has over how conflict will develop. This intervention initially entails a didactic element, in clarifying the four possible outcomes of conflict and adversity for your client; and rendering it clear to them that they have a choice about it:

1   *Destructive conflict:* This is the outcome of disaster that cannot be undone, utilised or metabolised. Ultimately, we all have to face a conflict with an irreversible, defeating outcome, the conflict with life. Which makes it all the more important to utilise all other conflict as well as we can. When working with conflict, your clients may need to hear and understand that, so that your work with them can move on to the next stage. For example, an executive, R., who has just missed their opportunity to claim a more senior role, may feel that this is the end of the road for them.

2   *Homeostatic conflict:* This is more often than not the wish we all share, upon experiencing loss, failure and disappointment: "I wish things could go back to the way they were". Notwithstanding that this is more often than not impossible, it is also worth considering how this deprives us from reaping the benefits of hardship; and eventually halts our evolution. Your clients need to understand this, so you can move on to the next stage. R., at this stage, could be experiencing a sense of relief that she is still with the company or that at least she has not taken a salary cut or lost her job. Though this stage signifies survival, homeostatic conflict is simply not good enough.

3   *Enhancing conflict:* This is where things start to become interesting. Existing competencies and expertise are improved and our client is now better endowed to deal with adversity. If R. wants to take advantage of the situation, she should carefully explore with her coach what it is that she could do even better from now on; and actively, methodically, apply it in pursuing her next objective. This stage is about *managing* conflict.

4   *Developmental conflict:* This is the final and most challenging phase of utilising conflict, since it calls for *a shift of paradigm*. At this stage, R. will not seek to re-establish the status quo; she will not even seek to improve or enhance it; she will seek to *define and determine* it. This means that instead of seeking solutions to the problem, she will seek opportunity. The coach can help by asking questions such as, "How does this setback allow you to turn your attention to something potentially more productive/profitable/rewarding/ambitious/meaningful?" Combined with good support on the accountability and influence fronts, this may enable your client to fly rather than just wander around. Please note that this takes guts from both sides and requires a quality coaching relation with a strong sense of rapport and resilience to risk. *This* is where the magic takes place. And unless the coach has tried it a few times for themself, then they had best stick to working on the previous three stages. One could argue that this is the optimum manifestation of Adversity Activated Development.

Self-awareness

It is a fundamental premise of this text that we cannot, and perhaps even should not, lead our clients further than where we are stationed. Even though some personal psychotherapy and an exploration of our internal existential challenges and conflicts would not go amiss, this is not an absolute prerequisite for coaching. Coaching is not psychotherapy; therefore, when we talk about self-awareness (both for the coach as well as for the client), we primarily refer to behavioural aspects. In other words, the coaching task should revolve, first and foremost, around discovering the impact that our client, and to be more precise their Persona (please see Chapter 5: Transformational leadership), has on those around them. Bridging this Persona with the client's Authentic Self (in other words, contributing towards their Individuation) is not a core coaching task. It is an advanced one.

We have so far explored the ways in which we can support our client's self-awareness and these are the creation of a customised 360-degree survey as well as the generation of data and provision of feedback based on the coaching relation (please see Chapter 2: Coaching methodology: "Data collection"; and Chapter 4: Fundamental skills: "Data generation"). Self-awareness can decisively contribute towards increasing our influence, since the discovery of our impact on others will align our intention with our behaviour and help us manage relations. Equally importantly, though, it can be a fundamental building block in the structure of resilience. For a start, knowing your blind and weak spots enables you to prepare for meeting challenges when they arise or extracting the right kind of support from your environment. For instance, understanding that you do not work well under pressure is vital information. You may choose to either work on improving that, or you may give yourself extra time to prepare. Resilience is not just about coping with the unexpected. Second, knowing the impact that you have on specific people around you will help you turn to the right individuals (key players) for support in times of crisis. There is nothing worse than feeling let down by your colleagues when you most need them. Finally, if you have taken the time and effort to discover what you are made of, you will be equipped with proactive pace; and this can probably be the most valuable asset during adversity.

For coaches, self-awareness ought to primarily revolve around having a fair understanding with regard to the impact we have on others, and secondarily a fair understanding of the factors that bring about this impact. Such factors include:

- our limiting beliefs (introjects as they are called in Gestalt theory; please see Chapter 4: Fundamental skills: "Generating data");
- our true knowledge, capacity and expertise;
- our overall attitude, principles and Epistemology.

It would be fair to question why such an attribute is necessary to an executive coach. The answer is that it can be of secondary importance to the executive coach who merely applies predesigned, behavioural interventions and relies on tools such as profilers to bring about some improvement for their client. After all, that is also the ideal way to avoid conflict. However, for the executive coach who relies on relational qualities, models and leads by example, and relies on who they are as much as what they do to support their client's transformation, finding ways to support an understanding of the self is vital. Some constructive ways to support our self-awareness is to receive and survive the kind of coaching we aim to give; to proactively and openly invite feedback from others with regard to the impact we have on them and the way they perceive us; or to secure supervision from a senior practitioner. Psychotherapy can also serve as a great way to align our "ins" with our "outs". However, this is optional and requires the choice of a therapist who can appreciate the professional reasons that have led us to their consulting room.

Naturally, our task with our clients also entails supporting their self-awareness. It is important that we start with a clear intention, so that we do not end up "therapising" and "analysing" them, for this would result in yet another, unwanted, conflict. Our primary quest in executive coaching is performance and not meaning; and this is what differentiates it from psychotherapy. Therefore, *even though it is worth understanding the "whys" of the past, we need to concentrate on the "hows" of the future.*

In summary, 360s, profilers and various tests are a good place to start. As indicated in Chapter 4 ("Tools: The customised 360-degree survey"), not only will you extract some useful content information, but you will also be able to observe your coachee's process. Providing feedback with regard to the impact they have on you, as well as inviting them to collect feedback from others, is naturally the best way to build self-awareness; as is the case with the coach. And as Sun Tzu (1995, p. 67) said, "If you know the enemy and know yourself, your victory will not stand in doubt; if you know heaven and know earth, you may make your victory complete".

Pace

Recent years have seen me make use of the term *pace* during coaching, training and consultation, equally if not more than terms such as feedback, rapport, empathy, etc. My personal and professional journey has confirmed that you can be talented, expert, smart, educated; yet, unless you can manage and determine your behaviour and its impact, you will not achieve victory, excellence, prosperity, success or whatever else your objective might be. Pace is a difficult one to define and it is by far the most "esoteric" of all five PRAID characteristics. It is esoteric, because in essence, it requires that we manage our internal processes, before allowing them to manifest externally. The definition I would, therefore, propose, is the following: "The ability and capacity to timely manage the urge for instant gratification, action or reaction, in a confident manner, as part of succeeding in greater objectives."

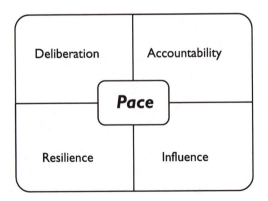

Figure 8.11 The PRAID Leadership Model – Pace

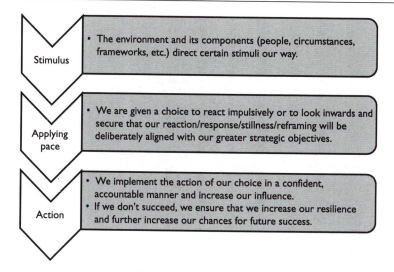

Figure 8.12 Pace

Stephen Covey's (1989, p. 65) first habit ("Be proactive" [not reactive]) echoes significant components of pace, since it invites leaders to take the initiative and determine their circumstances rather than find themselves *in a reactive position*. It also echoes existential processes, since every time we comply or react, our identity is determined by external factors rather than by us; and this creates yet another existential question: Can compulsion and spontaneity be authentic, especially in business? Think about it.

How do we apply pace though? In Figure 8.12, I present a linear, developmental process:

In addition, it is worth making a note of what *applying pace* ought to look and feel like, when successfully applied:

1 People and situations around us appear to go into slow motion, giving us enough time to make appropriate decisions and take focused action. This is the exact opposite of what happens when we are dealing with crisis, whereby everything around us seems to pick up speed, thus leaving us with little influence or control.
2 We seem to have the capacity to predict the course that several situations will take with a good rate of success and accuracy.
3 We have the capacity to influence the direction that a fair amount of situations will take with a good rate of success and accuracy.

As an avid motorsport and sports car enthusiast and frequent racetrack driver for the past two decades, the above process very much reminds me of trying to improve my lap time around a circuit. Accelerating, braking, choosing the racing

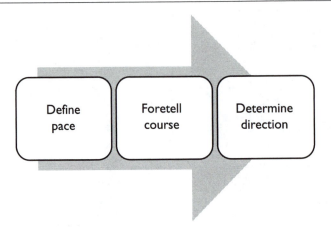

Figure 8.13 Applying pace

line, tactically slowing down to cool down the brakes and preserve my tyres, and, of course, preparing the car (sharpening the saw) and studying the circuit (managing information) in advance are all crucial factors in optimising performance. I would invite you to discover your own metaphor or visualisation that you can apply each time. In addition, there are some other activities and experiences that have supported me tremendously in avoiding compulsion and mastering my fate to the best of my ability. I outline those below and hope that you will be in a position to create and prescribe a similar routine for yourself and for your coachees:

- *Loss and personal challenges:* If we are still here, this means we have survived them all. We might as well apply Adversity Activated Development, since we cannot turn back time. The faith and belief that we will eventually sort things out, as we always have, are in themselves of vital importance in managing our internal pace and eventually our behaviour.
- *Martial arts:* As an Aikido practitioner for more than two decades, I have discovered that continuous practice enables one to press the "slow motion" button and "blend in" with the "opponent" in a way that renders the attack almost predictable. For those of you who have watched *The Matrix* (Lana and Lilly Wachowski, 1999), I can tell you that it is simply an exaggerated version of what really happens.
- *Free diving:* Holding your breath and trying to dive in, as deep as you can, demands that you can manage your biological processes with your brain. It is excellent practice for tranquillity, preparation, patience and mind over matter. An ideal setting in which to set your pace.
- *Music:* Playing the piano, especially when doing so within and for a group, requires that you can adjust your rhythm to match the circumstances, accommodate and include others. It is the perfect place to suboptimise and that greatly supports your ability to adjust pace, since you need to look both

inwards and outwards at the same time. It is also a solid contributor to individuating, being yourself whilst connecting.

- *Reflective Practice:* With a background in psychotherapy, there have been several occasions on which I have been hard pushed to provide relief, answers or solutions for my clients, perhaps in an even more pressing context than coaching can ever reproduce. At times, I have compulsively jumped in for the rescue; at other times, I have managed to keep my cool; and from time to time, I have jumped out and redirected the conversation. Self-awareness, supervision, practice and continuous professional development have supported my growth and development. However, developing pace is what has enabled me to work, for the most part, on the boundary, without either jumping in to rescue my client (for example, by providing reassurance, answers or solutions) or jumping out to rescue myself (for example, by relying on method, tools or technique). Needless to say, failure is frequent and therefore resilience is supported day in, day out.

I have relied heavily on personal disclosure during this section, since pace is a highly internalised, experiential, personal aspect for each one of us. It is a personal, *transformational* journey and even though the destination may appear similar, what will get us there differs greatly for each one of us. I hope I have taken a step forward in modelling it through stories and examples and you are now in a position to start modelling it through your behaviour and disposition to your coachees.

> Utilise resources and influence; be responsible for yourself and accountable to others; establish your circumstances; don't protest; be deliberate.

Chapter 9

Coaching for impact

The tools that the executive coach will employ will only be as effective as they are. However, it is important that some form of map is available. You may never need to use it; however, knowing that it is there will provide you with much-needed confidence in kicking off the engagement, moving things forward when the work is at an impasse, collecting valuable information and forming a rapport-based relationship.

This chapter will cover eight specific coaching questions and interventions that I have personally found to be serving all of the above during the past two decades.

1. Who are you?

Contrary to the other seven interventions (which I may from time to time just neglect altogether), I never fail to kick off the preliminary meeting or first session with this question. It is both as unexpected as it is revealing. The client will usually respond by providing their job description or, at best, their family status. The seasoned, curious coach will probe further by thanking the coachee for telling them what *they do* and repeating the question. A fine way of creating context and direction is to ask what an honest friend would say about them, if they were trying to set them up for a romantic relationship with another good friend of theirs. There is some boldness and some risk in this, and risk is the building block for rapport. You are looking to collect information with regard to their primary characteristics and their self-perception, both negative and positive. Are they ambitious, stubborn, flexible, compulsive, introvert? Recording this response will come in very handy in the course of the coaching relation, since it will enable a deep exploration of the discrepancies of the client's self-perception and other people's perception of them, especially when combined with a customised 360.

This question, which also introduces some performance-enhancing existential elements to the work, can be developed further using a variety of creative techniques. For example, I have found that asking my client to come up with the four qualities that are of paramount importance to them, and then exploring which aspects, activities and tasks of their daily work or personal life fall within or in between these categories, can generate exceptional circumstances for calibration.

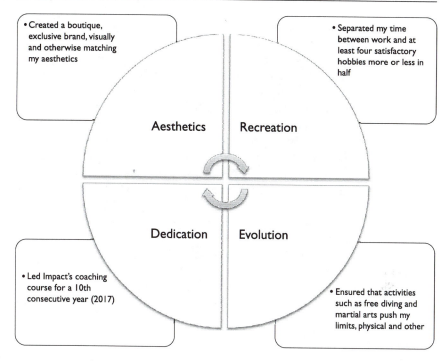

Figure 9.1 Coupled with PRAID (my professional Leadership Model), DARE serves as my set of personal, applicable values

In Figure 9.1, I share what this looked like, when I applied it for myself, conveniently applying the acronym DARE, with one activity example per category.

Furthermore, you can run wild with it; for example, by creating similar charts with regard to the characteristics that you want those around you to have, the features that you would like your workplace to have and many more. It would be fair to say that in itself, this journey could prove sufficiently productive for the whole duration of a six-session coaching engagement. However, it is worth having access to even more. So let's look at intervention number 2.

2. Why not you?

Four possible outcomes: Win–Win, Win–Lose, Lose–Lose and No Deal. The latter we discount or take personally; look for your energy, time and resources there.

It works well to take your coachee by surprise and to stimulate their mind. Contrary to the recent trend of focusing on the positive, glorifying and excusing failure and refusing to take responsibility for our progress (or lack of it), the seasoned coach should not shy away from identifying challenges, obstacles and shortcomings; thus supporting their client in neutralising, overcoming or even utilising them. People need to know exactly what stops them from being as successful as they can. The usual responses will mostly revolve around the client indicating that there are two primary reasons for not fulfilling their potential: The first one is that they are "too nice" to claim what they deserve or to promote themselves. The second one has to do with the fact that others don't understand, appreciate or support them. What they are effectively saying is that they are victims with no influence, whose narcissism does not allow them to make the effort to progress. It is important, if this is the case with your client, that you find productive and non-offensive ways of challenging this. A fine way to go about it is to work on identifying their limiting beliefs and introjects. These may include: "I cannot control my environment", "I can never master enough influence to change my own and others' circumstances", "Everyone is out to get me" and many more. In addition to challenging these notions and devising strategies for overcoming them, it may serve to conduct some preliminary, exploratory work, with regard to how they came to develop these beliefs, without, of course, venturing into oceans of deep psychology.

3. How do you lose and gain influence?

> Don't care much as to why you couldn't make it work; very interested to hear more about how we will.

Once again, the subject of influence is of paramount importance on every level of the coaching engagement, including the technical. This third intervention entails some didactic work from the coach's side, taking the coachee over the parameters that will define and determine the influence they will have over people and circumstances. As indicated and analysed, especially in Chapter 8, influence depends on managing information and relations and securing access to resources. Your task at this stage is to, primarily, discover your coachee's *Distance Regulators*. Distance Regulators are the things we do and the things we are that keep people at a distance from us. This distance is very costly, since it jeopardises our access to alliances, information, key players and eventually influence.

There are two major types of Distance Regulator: The first one entails the tactical and conscious behaviours and choices that we apply daily, in order to avoid and evade what we consider to be a hassle, a burden or an unnecessary overhead: not picking up a call, not responding to emails, procrastinating, avoiding a meeting or calling in sick are examples of such behaviours. The coach's job here is to briefly go over such behaviours with the client and assess what the P & L (profit and loss) account consequently looks like. I know it from myself; for the most part, if I consciously and tactically shy away from something, it usually means that the benefit

I expect to get from it does not match the effort I am required to put into it. In my opinion, *Conscious Tactical Distance Regulators* (CTDR) *are not really an issue*.

What is an issue are the *Subconscious Strategic Distance Regulators*. These *SSDR* are the chronic (and therefore strategic in nature) barriers we place in our connection with others, with the aim of maintaining our safe distance. Permanently. Forever. Unlike *CTDR*, these patterns are, more often than not, subconscious, or at least we are unaware of the impact they have on others and therefore how we are perceived. These may include our predisposition to protest or come across as a victim, passive aggression, stubbornness, a tendency to be controlling, inconsistency, unavailability, exhaustion, arrogance, bitterness, an inclination to be judgemental and many more. In the context of aligning our intention with the impact we have on others, it is important that we try to shed light on at least the fundamental SSDR that our coachee suffers from. In addition to relying on carefully designed and focused customised 360s, it is also important that we observe and record our countertransferential reactions (please see Chapter 4: Fundamental skills: "Generating data"; "Psychodynamic competencies and the use of self"), which we can then make available to our client in the form of carefully constructed and delivered phenomenological feedback.

Case study 12: The blond terrorist

Have you ever noticed how you tend to avoid certain people?

Worse yet, come to think of it, do you think you avoid certain people without even noticing?

Even worse; do you think people perhaps avoid you, consciously or subconsciously?

Several years back, I was consulting for a medium-size company in technology. Usually, when I engage in projects, I aim to establish contact with most people either by simply greeting them, being actively curious about what they are doing and who they are or semi-formally spending time with them in the context of collecting data and engaging them. I more or less succeeded in deliberately establishing contact with most members of staff. However, as the weeks went by, I noticed that I never stopped by the office of a certain individual and secretly hoped that she would also not approach me, so much so that I almost experienced fear every time I walked past her in the corridor. Fortunately, she also did a great job of avoiding eye or other contact, so I managed to get away with it for several months. I gradually became conscious of what was going on and challenged myself on it. I recollected every time I had observed her engage in any type of interaction and realised that on every single occasion, she was busy either protesting about one "unfair" thing or another, being cynical, ironic and overall a ball of negative energy. I decided to ask the CEO what he thought of this particular individual, and unsurprisingly, he said that he rarely collaborated or even communicated with her. For the next few weeks, I observed the situation. People would either avoid her completely or collude with her to engage in relentless nagging, pessimistic rumbling and general criticism before disappearing. As a matter of fact, within a 4-metre radius of where she sat, silence prevailed. It was, however, a very angry silence and even a non-empathic individual such as myself could pick that up. Effectively, the executive had determined the distance that others would keep from her as well as what they would do in the event that they wanted to make some contact. Indeed, she managed to keep herself in a safe space by terrorising, intimidating and distancing others. At the same time, she also managed to keep herself on the margin and be a passive recipient of other people's decisions instead of a proactive determiner of her fate and the fate of others. Very convenient for protesting; not so convenient for progressing. The executive left the company, to everyone's relief. Coincidentally, I have just discovered that she has also been fired from her next job. Her manager's final words were, "Everyone wants you to go".

4. Why you?

Upon identifying and neutralising limitations and obstacles, it is time to empower your client. "Why you?" is a good place to begin unravelling the thread of power. After all, the coach is not a troubleshooter, they are a performance enhancer. It is vital that you invite your client to put sentiments of pretentious humbleness aside and together explore the following: *What makes them better than others? What has brought them this far? What makes them stand out? Why would someone, anyone, "put their money" on them?*

There is little point in allocating energy and resources in improving areas where your coachee is not naturally inclined to provide an outstanding performance. At best, and as already specified, you and your client should work on neutralising severe performance deterrents. Invite them to invest in their areas of strength; they are the ones that require the shortest travelling distance. Cover it. Shamelessly.

5. What purpose does this serve?

Everything we do or don't do serves a purpose. The more we understand about it, the more we influence outcomes. This applies for well-intended, productive behaviour and choices. It applies even more to unproductive, seemingly barren patterns, such as the aforementioned Distance Regulators. This is Shadow territory (please see Chapter 5: Transformational leadership). And it needs to be explored and integrated, in order to be managed.

This is a question that may lead our client into a short-circuit: "How can unproductive behaviour be serving a purpose?" The response usually is, "It does not serve any, it is simply wrong." At this stage, the preparatory work you have conducted should pay off. If you have succeeded in identifying introjects (limiting beliefs) and Distance Regulators, then exploring the purpose they serve should follow on more smoothly.

The primary purpose served by distancing, unproductive behaviour is the maintaining of distance and safety. There are, however, a plethora of other, secondary sub-scripts, which guide the way we position ourselves within systems; and eventually our actions and behaviour. Such scripts (Epistemology, according to Renos Papadopoulos) include an assumed victim position, a sense of entitlement, a tendency to be reactive, different, to stand out, to remain on the margins, feel "special", "unique", "better", "justified", etc. All behaviour and all choices serve a purpose.

6. Tell me about your Persona

Each and every erroneous Persona you have trialled is a springboard towards authenticity. Individuate; deductively; unashamedly; unapologetically.

Chapter 5 (Transformational leadership) explored Jung's concept of the Persona, in the context of executive coaching. The Persona is the mask we wear, the character and identity we assume to blend in. It contains both pathological and unproductive elements as well as healthy components of adaptability. The extent to which it is authentic, and the extent to which authenticity is related to successful leadership, depend on individual cases. If we have nurtured a Persona that facilitates our growth and the growth of those around us, then, personally, I consider the quest for authenticity to be of secondary importance. After all, many would argue, we are what we repeatedly do, and it is near impossible to distinguish between the components that form part of the true self and the components that belong to the false self. After all, Winnicott, who actually coined the terms true and false self, indicated that "the self has an innermost core that remains incommunicado" (cited by Gomez, 1998, p. 214). The Persona is not necessarily part of a false self, or at least it shouldn't be; the Persona ought to be part of the effective self and we should be at ease with it. If we think about it, in archetypal terms, every superhero, from Spiderman to Batman, acts in the context of their Persona when they wear a mask, with Superman being an interesting exception, since his authentic self is a superhero and his Persona a mere mortal.

In any case, this is a discussion worth having with your coachee. To what extent does their Persona facilitate and accommodate other people's needs or their own fear-based need to be accepted and included; and to what extent does it warrant communication, collaboration and general synergy? Whatever the answer may be, the coach's job is to facilitate a balanced integration and support the management of feelings of guilt (on the one hand) and feelings of anger (on the other). You can't be an Adapted or a Natural Child (as proposed by Eric Berne in his Transactional Analysis theory in the 1950s) all the time. Too much adaptation, and we risk losing contact with ourselves. At the same time, giving in to our natural urges is likely to cause major grievances in our relation with others. Some key points to consider and cover are the following:

- How do you want to be perceived by others?
- What is the P & L (profit and loss) of your current Persona?
- Who do you, eventually, want to be?

These questions will most likely provide conflicting answers. Once you have those, the serious work begins.

7. Let's do feedback

> If you are smart enough to give feedback, you should be smart enough to propose alternatives.

The use of feedback in the art of coaching has been extensively covered throughout this text, with an emphasis on using customised 360s to generate data and feedback as well as phenomenological feedback (Chapter 4: Fundamental skills: "Giving and receiving feedback"). The intention of providing our clients with feedback is to align their intention with their impact, thus deliberately supporting their influence. Coaches provide feedback based on content; seasoned coaches provide feedback on process, such as repeated patterns, characterological traits, limiting beliefs, etc. (Chapter 4: Fundamental skills: "Generating data"). The impact of receiving feedback depends on the intention of the person giving it (for instance, a coach who consciously, or unconsciously, wishes to punish or dominate the coachee, will most likely create trauma rather than progress or collude in a repetitive, sadomasochistic pattern that the coachee is familiar with); the timing (which is all about pace, as presented in Chapter 8); the quality and rapport of the coaching relation; and, of course, the coach's expertise and experience.

Providing a client with feedback is an ongoing intervention and can (and perhaps should) start unravelling as early as the preliminary meeting or the first session. As a matter of fact, I feel that failing to provide feedback at an early stage of the coaching engagement will diminish the coachee's interest; I therefore try to ensure that my clients know a little something, with regard to the impact they have on me and the way I perceive them, as early as possible. As with all risks, this tends to escalate as the coaching progresses and towards the end of the coaching engagement, having had an opportunity to observe the forest and not just the trees, if I am not in a position to provide comprehensive, meaningful feedback, I feel like I am missing something; which in itself is useful information and perhaps indicative of a specific countertransference (please see Chapter 4: Fundamental skills: "Generating data"). Finally, *feedback should aim to support and challenge in equal measure*. Too much support, and the client's transformational pace is slowed down; too much challenge and the coaching relation becomes punitive or antagonistic. Of all coaching arts, collecting and generating the information, and rendering it useful and actionable for your client, is the finest.

8. What is it all about?

At the end of the day, this is the most important question of them all. Despite it originating from an existential rather than a business perspective, when answered, it can be the ultimate performance enhancer. At the end of the coaching engagement, our client should have some idea as to why they do what they do, why they want to achieve what they want to achieve and how all that forms part of their story and *legacy*. Themes and patterns should be clearer; findings and decision-making data should entail a personal, meaningful element that is congruent with who the client is or wants to be; or wants to become. The conflicts, polarities, discrepancies and contradictions that they play host to should now be more visible. The work should have helped them assume responsibility (accountability, as discussed in Chapter 8: Leading with PRAID) for a successful future, rather than focusing on how others contributed to a failed past.

Since this final chapter is meant to aid you as a hands-on guide, I will close it off by sharing the actual questions that may serve as an appropriate closure to the coaching journey. Needless to say, before directing them to anyone else, it is of paramount importance that you have some answers for yourself:

* "What have you discovered, which was unknown to you before?"
* "What has been confirmed for you?"
* "What will be your next steps?"

. . . "What is it all about?"

Bibliography

Berne, E. 1964. *Games People Play: The Psychology of Human Relationships*. New York: Grove Press.

Bion, W.R. 1959. *Attacks on Linking: Second Thoughts*. London: Heinemann.

Block, P. 2000. *Flawless Consulting: A Guide to Getting your Expertise Used*. San Francisco, CA: Jossey-Bass/Pfeiffer.

Bluckert, P. 2006. *Psychological Dimensions of Executive Coaching*. Maidenhead, UK: Open University Press.

Clarkson, P. 1993. *On Psychotherapy*. London: Whurr Publishers.

Clarkson, P. 1994. *The Achilles Syndrome*. Shaftesbury, UK: Element.

Clavell, J. 1981. Foreword. In Sun Tzu, *The Art of War*. London: Hodder & Stoughton.

Covey, S.R. 1989. *The 7 Habits of Highly Effective People*. New York: Free Press.

Covey, S.M.R. (with R.R. Merrill) 2006. *The Speed of Trust*. New York: Free Press.

Dunne, C. 2000. *Carl Jung: Wounded Healer of the Soul*. London: Continuum.

Goleman, D. 1995. *Emotional Intelligence: Why it Can Matter More than IQ*. New York: Bantam Books.

Gomez, L. 1998. *An Introduction to Object Relations*. London: Free Association Books.

Guevara, E. 2009. *Guerrilla Warfare*. London: Harper Perennial.

Jung, C.G. 1964 [1923]. *Psychological Types or the Psychology of Individuation*. London: Routledge & Kegan Paul.

Jung, C.G. 1966. *The Practice of Psychotherapy*. 2nd edition. Princeton, NJ: Princeton University Press.

Jung, C.G. 1968. *The Archetypes and the Collective Unconscious*. 2nd edition. London: Routledge.

Jung, C.G. 1973 [1960]. *Synchronicity: An Acausal Connecting Principle*. Princeton, NJ: Princeton/Bollingen.

Jung, C.G. 1990 [1964]. *Man and his Symbols*. London: Penguin Arkana.

Jung, C.G. 1995 [1963]. *Memories, Dreams, Reflections*. London: Fontana Press.

Karpman, S. 1968. Fairy tales and script drama analysis. *Transactional Analysis Bulletin*, 26(7): 39–43.

Kemp, S. 2017. The incredible growth of the internet over the past five years – explained in detail. We Are Social, 14 March. Retrieved from https://wearesocial.com/blog/2017/03/incredible-growth-internet-past-five-years-explained-detail

Kern, H. 2003. *Discipline: Six Steps to Unleashing your Hidden Potential*. United States: 1st Books Library.

Klein, M. 1946. Notes on some schizoid mechanisms. *International Journal of Psychoanalysis*, 27: 99–110.

Machiavelli, N. 2007. *Il Principe*. 20th edition. Athens: Patakis.

Mollon, P. 1993. *The Fragile Self*. London: Whurr Publishers.

Neumann, J.E., Kellner, K. and Dawson-Shepherd, A. (Eds) 1997. *Developing Organisational Consultancy*. London: Routledge.

Nevis, E.C. 1987. *Organizational Consulting: A Gestalt Approach*. Santa Cruz, CA: GestaltPress.

Nietzsche, F. 1969. *Thus Spoke Zarathustra*. London: Penguin.

Papadopoulos, R. 2006. *The Handbook of Jungian Psychology: Theory, Practice and Applications*. London & New York: Routledge.

Papadopoulos R. and Saayman G. 1991. *Jung in Modern Perspective*. Bridport, UK: Prism Press.

Papadopoulos, R. 2007. Refugees, trauma and Adversity-Activated Development. *European Journal of Psychotherapy & Counselling*, 9(3): 301–312.

Peltier, B. 2001. *The Psychology of Executive Coaching: Theory and Application*. New York: Routledge.

Rogers, C. 1959. A theory of therapy, personality and interpersonal relationships as developed in the client-centered framework. In S. Koch (Ed.), *Psychology: A Study of a Science. Vol. 3: Formulations of the Person and the Social Context*. New York: McGraw Hill.

Rogers, C.R. 1961. *On Becoming a Person: A Therapist's View of Psychotherapy*. Boston, MA: Houghton Mifflin.

Rogers, C.R. 1975. Empathic: An unappreciated way of being. *The Counselling Psychologist*, 5(2): 2–10.

Rowe, C.E. and Mac Isaac, D.S. 2000. *Empathic Attunement: The "Technique" of Psychoanalytic Self Psychology*. Northvale, NJ: Jason Aronson Inc. Publishers.

Schneider, W.E. 1997. Aligning strategy, culture and leadership. In J.E. Neumann, K. Kellner and A. Dawson-Shepherd, (Eds), *Developing Organisational Consultancy*. London: Routledge, pp. 250–266.

Seneca the Younger. First century AD. *Epistulae Morales ad Lucilium* (*Moral Letters to Lucilius*). Letter LXXI: On the supreme good.

Storr, A. 1995. *Jung*. London: Fontana Press.

Sun Tzu. 1995. *The Art of War*. London: Hodder & Stoughton.

Tsunetomo, Y. 1979. *Hagakure: The Book of the Samurai*. Tokyo: Kodansha.

UN Population Division. World Population Prospects. Retrieved from https://esa.un.org/unpd/wpp/

Von Bertalanffy, L. 1968. *General System Theory*. New York: George Braziller.

Von Clausewitz, C. 2007. *On War*. New York: Oxford University Press.

Von Franz, M. 2000. *The Problem of Puer Aeternus*. Toronto, ON: Inner City Books.

Wachowski, Lana and Wachowski, Lilly. 1999. *The Matrix* (motion picture). Burbank, CA: Warner Bros.

Whitmore, J. 2009. *Coaching for Performance*. 4th edition. London and Boston, MA: Nicholas Brealey Publishing.

Wikipedia. 2016. Digital Revolution. Retrieved from https://en.wikipedia.org/wiki/Digital_Revolution

Wikipedia. 2017. Perception. Retrieved from https://en.wikipedia.org/wiki/Perception

Index